TEENAGE TATA

VOICES OF YOUNG FATHERS IN SOUTH AFRICA

Sharlene Swartz & Arvin Bhana

Save the Children
Sweden

HSRC PRESS

Published by HSRC Press
Private Bag X9182, Cape Town, 8000, South Africa
www.hsrcpress.ac.za

First published 2009

ISBN (soft cover) 978-0-7969-2287-8
ISBN (pdf) 978-0-7969-2288-5

© 2009 Human Sciences Research Council and Save the Children Sweden

Copyedited by Lee Smith
Typeset by Simon van Gend
Cover design by Jenny Young
Printed by Logo Print, Cape Town

Distributed in Africa by Blue Weaver
Tel: +27 (0) 21 701 4477; Fax: +27 (0) 21 701 7302
www.oneworldbooks.com

Distributed in Europe and the United Kingdom by Eurospan Distribution Services (EDS)
Tel: +44 (0) 20 7240 0856; Fax: +44 (0) 20 7379 0609
www.eurospanbookstore.com

Distributed in North America by Independent Publishers Group (IPG)
Call toll-free: (800) 888 4741; Fax: +1 (312) 337 5985
www.ipgbook.com

Contents

Tables and figures

Tables

Figures

Foreword

In late 2003 the Fatherhood Project was initiated in the Child, Youth, Family and Social Development (CYFSD) programme at the Human Sciences Research Council. The project developed from a series of consultations and finally a regional meeting to discuss the 2002 publication of several shocking cases of infant and child rape in South Africa. These included the reports in newspapers such as the Sunday Times covering the ongoing rape and eventual death of two-year-old Thendo Nenzhelele, the rape and sodomy of nine-month-old Baby Tshepang, and the abuse and suffering of countless other young children. My work on a chapter in *Sexual Abuse of Young Children in southern Africa* (Richter et al, 2004), which takes these terrible assaults as a starting point for an evaluation of the problem of child sexual abuse, also brought back memories of an earlier case in which I had been involved.

The material was deeply disturbing. I found myself losing attention in the company of men, and watching them – men I was talking to, men walking past and especially men in close proximity to children. Questions ran through my head. Could this man rape a child, could that man penetrate a baby, could yet another lure a toddler into a dark space? Simultaneously, the gentle protectiveness and integrity of men in my own life kept pulling me from these dark thoughts. My father, my brothers, my husband, my son – none of them could ever do such things. I knew this.

In watching men, however, I started to notice something else, a part of men that seemed invisible in the public domain. Men could lovingly touch a baby, hold their arms around their daughter in devoted absorption, reach out to gently guide a child from a threat, smile in captivation while watching a boisterous child. What I was noticing was fathering – soft, caring feelings and actions toward children; protection, even when expressed as rowdy play.

I could find little in the literature from South Africa, or even from Africa, which examined fatherhood as a core identity of men, or as a repertoire of socialised emotionality and behaviour. Instead, the public media was, and remains, replete with reports of men's selfishness (spending money on cigarettes and alcohol and, at the high end, on golf and expensive 'toys'), their neglect of their children (failing to pay maintenance or spending long hours at work), their uncontrolled sexuality (multiple, superficial partnerships), their violent behaviour, and their abuse, including rape and murder, of women and children.

Alongside the work on child sexual abuse in the Fatherhood Project, Robert Morrell and I began to conceive of a book that was eventually published under the title Baba: Men and Fatherhood in South Africa (Richter & Morrell 2006), a compilation of what was known and what still needs to be explored about this significant topic. We approached people whom we knew were working in this field, and they led us to others. A fascinating combination of theory, empirical investigation, policy analysis and advocacy emerged. But it was obvious that much more needs to be done.

We used the term baba (isiZulu for 'father') as the organising motif for our book, just as Sharlene Swartz and Arvin Bhana use tata (the isiXhosa equivalent) for this book. Across the world, intimate family relationships have evolved around the care and protection of children, yet children continue to suffer from abuse and neglect. For this reason, and many others, there is something vitally important about studying what it means to be a father, and/or to father others. Baba: Men and Fatherhood in South

Africa opened doors and windows, and shed light on some unexplored and generally dark spaces. In doing so, it demonstrated that the ability to provide materially for children lies at the core of our current understanding of fatherhood. As Ramphele notes in Steering by the Stars (Ramphele 2002), when men cannot provide money, food, accommodation, school fees, health care, and the little things that bring joy to children, their sense of themselves as fathers, and as men, is severely challenged – sometimes to the point of abandonment.

Sharlene and Arvin have set off from this point in their research, and pose questions about what it means to be chronically poor, with few prospects of providing materially for dependents, and to become a father while still a teenager. Their analyses are deep and expansive, addressing the circumstances in which impoverished young men become fathers, how they disclose this fact to family and friends, the ways in which their ambitions for education and work change their relationship with the mother of their child, and their own engagement with their child.

Using 'snowball sampling' (Goodman 1961) to find young men who acknowledge being fathers, Sharlene and Arvin draw out their voices through several encounters within the study. The monograph is beautifully written and well illustrated with the words of the protagonists. What beams through is the responsibility young men feel towards their children, and their emotional investment in them. But what is also evident is that these young men have very few options for realising this sense of responsibility, or for contributing meaningfully to the material well-being of their children. The young men point clearly to ways in which they need help to become the fathers they want to be.

It is plain that this study will be a landmark on the path towards the development of innovative programmes to assist young fathers. Adults grieve that they never knew their fathers, and children long to know their fathers: simultaneously, fathers regret that they never knew their children or bonded with their children's children. This cycle of absent fathers can be interrupted if young men receive the support and assistance they need. But we also need to change our understanding of what it is to be a father, and put material provision in perspective so that other aspects of fathering can come to the fore – aspects that young men, poor men, men with disabilities and unemployed men can fulfil. Of course, there is a bottom line to provision by any parent, but when children are asked the meaning of fatherhood, they make it clear that simply having a father who cares about them, who is 'there' and who gives them affection and direction, is the most important aspect of fatherhood to them (Richter & Morrell 2006).

I am very proud that Sharlene Swartz and Arvin Bhana have continued and so impressively extended CYFSD's work in this field. Continuity in scholarship, from one group to another linked group, is not common in South Africa but is desperately needed. This monograph not only demonstrates how an important area of study can be expanded and taken in new directions, but also illustrates the benefit of networks in research. We all look forward to the next steps by this group.

Linda Richter
Executive Director
Child, Youth, Family and Social Development
Human Sciences Research Council

Preface

This study, funded by Save the Children Sweden, provides an in-depth portrait of the experiences of impoverished young men in the South African context who became fathers as teenagers. Specifically, it answers two closely related research questions: 'How do young men living in poverty, and those involved with them, *experience* fatherhood?' and 'What are the factors that *help* or *hinder* young men's engagement in the parenting of their children?'

Part 1 describes the reason for the study: the dearth of data on young fathers in the developing world, as well as the limited focus predicting numerous negative life outcomes on becoming a young father, instead of studies that focus on the phenomenon of *being a young father in an impoverished environment*. In Part 1 we also describe the strategy of using community informants to recruit participants for the study, and document the use of a pair of semi-structured interviews and innovative participatory strategies. These include inviting participants to interview members of their social networks and to comment on the draft report as expert consultants at the conclusion of the study. This section also describes in detail the 27 young men from Langa and Bonteheuwel in Cape Town, and Cato Manor, Bonella and Mayville in Durban, who, while not a statistically representative sample, include sufficient diversity to reflect the experiences of many young fathers who live in impoverished communities in South Africa.

Part 2 records the experiences of these young fathers, grouped into four main themes: coming to terms with being a young father; young fathers' perspectives on good fathering; young fathers' influences, practices and relationships; and the meaning of sexual health for impoverished young men. Key findings in Chapter 3 therefore include the strong emotional response that young fathers portray in response to the news of their impending fatherhood; the way in which they articulate the meaning of 'responsibility' in relation to their child; the multiple reasons for having a child at a young age – including, but not limited to, the role of alcohol and the lack of condom use in their peer group; and the multiple ways in which fatherhood has changed their lives and the nature of their primary relationships with partners, parents, school and community.

More specifically, in Chapter 4 young fathers offer their own analysis of what it means to be a *good* father – being present, talking and providing. For many, having had an *absent* father themselves, they are more determined to be a *present* father for their own children. The chapter also juxtaposes young men's contentions that having had a 'present' father who talked to them was the most important aspect of their own experience of being fathered with what they believe *now*: that providing financially is the only authentic (or at least the most important) action that fathers must play in the lives of their children. This anomaly of discounting presence and participation in favour of financial provision is further interrogated and leads to a discussion of the role of culture and family on fathering attitudes and practices.

Consequently, Chapter 5 focuses on the role of culture and traditional practices around childbearing and forming households; the relationship between the young father and the mother of his child as the fulcrum around which parental participation occurs (including the role of her family); and the prominent role played by young fathers' mothers – both as an enabling and a disenabling force in her son's life. Particular attention is paid to issues of childcare, mediation, mothers' roles in termination of pregnancy decisions, and financial provision for the ongoing education of children born to young fathers.

In Chapter 6, young men speak frankly about *reasons* for multiple concurrent partnerships (MCPs) and the meaning of condom-less sex. While both practices place these young men at high risk of contracting HIV and other sexually transmitted infections, young men provide compelling data regarding condoms as the currency of trust and fidelity; the choice they face between becoming *gangstas* or *pleyas*; and also the emotional issues of pain, attention-seeking and lack of meaningful attachment associated with having MCPs. This chapter concludes by reflecting on the lack of sexual health services available to young men, as well as the current weaknesses perceived by these young men in the sex education they receive.

In Part 3, the main findings of the study are distilled into 10 factors that either hinder or encourage young men's sexual health and participation in the fathering of their children. The 10 hindering factors include the cultural measure of money being equated with responsibility; young men's view of money dominating over practices and qualities; frequent rejection by the mother of their child's family; high unemployment rates; MCPs among young men; ignorance about basic biology and contraception; a foreshortened view of the future; the way in which parents commandeer young fathers' responsibilities; the common geographical separation between father and child; and the widespread failure of services and sex education for these young men. The 10 enabling features include young fathers' strong but silent sense of responsibility; their often unheard accounts of emotional engagement with their children; the motivating power of young fathers' own absent fathers on their parenting intentions; their clear ability to articulate the qualities of good fathers and practices of good fathering; the strong roles of their mothers in young fathers' lives; the effects of being welcomed by the mother of their child's family; the desire for sex education and mentoring by peers and family members (especially male family members); young fathers' clear aspirations for future involvement with their child; a clear recognition of the help they need; and the frequency and willingness with which young fathers participate in HIV testing and begin to use contraceptives following the birth of their child.

Attention is also given to young fathers' recommendations about sexual health and well-being to other young fathers in particular, and to young men living in impoverished communities in general. These recommendations include better sex education, especially from fathers and other male family members; more structured leisure opportunities; the importance of keeping young fathers in school; and better skills development for young fathers, especially around emotional skills – including coping with stress and building a relationship with the mother of their child's family. Young fathers' advice to young men in general about sexual health and well-being centred around condom use; not mixing sex and alcohol; understanding the consequences of having a child as a young man; and the importance of education and employment for fatherhood. Notably absent was any advice or recommendations around how the mother of their child should be treated or around limiting MCPs.

Finally, Part 3 concludes by discussing the use of social networking interviews as the basis for an intervention with young fathers to help them create closer ties with the mother of their child's family and other members of their social network. These interviews also proved helpful to young fathers as they confronted the demanding and competing requirements of their culture (especially amongst isiXhosa and isiZulu young men) in their efforts to be and remain engaged with their child.

Acknowledgements

This study has been a collaborative effort. While Sharlene Swartz conducted most of the interviews, enormous thanks are due to Lynn Hendricks, a master's intern in the Cape Town office of the Child, Youth, Family and Social Development (CYFSD) research programme of the Human Sciences Research Council, for interviewing the young men from Bonteheuwel, and to Nomhle Ndimande, a research assistant in the Pretoria office of CYFSD, who interviewed the young men in KwaZulu-Natal.

Also key in this study has been our team of community informants, who identified young fathers and encouraged them to participate in the study so that teenage pregnancy in South Africa may finally include in its focus young men's stories. To Siya Dlokweni, Atikah Ismail, Ntomboyise Mashwa, Lucky Mvundla, Selvy Nkasawe and Mandla Yeki – a huge vote of thanks. A special word of thanks also to interview transcribers Selvy Nkasawe, Liesl Stewart and Maurietta Stewart for the care with which they captured nuance and emotion, and for engaging in the debrief with young fathers with careful and thoughtful responses. Also to Velephi Riba from Save the Children Sweden, and Professor Linda Richter and Dr Saadhna Panday who made valuable comments on the draft report.

Finally, to the brave, engaging young fathers who told difficult, intimate and painful stories with a candour that has hugely enriched this report – thank you so much. And especially for your willingness to engage with the completed report, respond to it, add to it, and clear up misunderstandings and get the details right – thank you for allowing your stories to enrich our lives and, hopefully, inform our policies.

Terminology

Racial terminology is problematic in South Africa. Throughout this report, whenever an ethnic or 'racial' description is referred to, it is enclosed in inverted commas. This is done to convey the artificiality of the concept of 'race' and the terms 'black', 'white', 'coloured' and 'Indian'. These concepts are not biologically fixed; rather, they refer to the legacy of the apartheid system of racial classification as defined by the South African Population Registration Act (No. 30) of 1950. At the moment in South Africa, it is still standard practice to use these (or other) descriptors in order to call attention to continuing inequalities and their effects. Some use 'African' or 'black African' instead of 'black'; some capitalise both terms; and yet others use 'black' to include people described as 'coloured'. Our use of these terms is pragmatic: it is used for descriptive purposes and does not imply endorsement of any of these classifications. When quoting a source, we leave the descriptor as found in the text. When quoting research respondents, we leave the descriptors without inverted commas for ease of reading.

Measurement of impoverishment: For the purposes of this study, 'poverty' refers to the 47.1 per cent of the South African population who live below the 'upper bound' poverty line of R593 per capita per month as defined by Statistics South Africa in 2008 and reported in Armstrong et al. (2008: 8). By 'race' group, the proportion of those who are poor is: 'black' 93.3 per cent, 'coloured' 6.3 per cent, 'Indian' 0.4 per cent and 'white' 0.1 per cent (Armstrong et al. 2008: 12).

Tata is the isiXhosa word for father. Like the isiZulu term *baba*, it is a polite form of address to an older African man, whether or not there is a blood relationship. We have called this book *Teenage Tata* to show how young fatherhood in South Africa is frequently a family, rather than only an individual, phenomenon, as well as to show continuity with the book *Baba: Men and Fatherhood in South Africa* (Richter & Morrell 2006), whose pioneering work inspired this study.

Glossary of colloquial, isiZulu and isiXhosa terms

amandla	power (isiXhosa)
baba	father, often a term of respect for a non-relative (isiZulu)
dagga	marijuana, ganja (colloquial)
eish	an interjection used to express surprise, disbelief, shock or exasperation. Originally a transliteration from isiXhosa but now common in South African English.
gangsta	gangster, gang member, also used for criminal
hlonipha	respect (isiXhosa)
ibari	someone newly arrived from a rural area, greenhorn, 'out of style', sometimes equivalent to 'mommy's baby' (isiXhosa). Plural – *iibari*.
ikasi	township, location (similar to 'the hood', 'ghetto', 'el barrio', 'council estates', 'banlieue', 'slum', 'favela') (isiXhosa). Sometimes used interchangeably with *kasi* and *ekasi*.
ikrwala	term for newly initiated young men, in the period while they are wearing their suits as a sign that they've just completed their *ulwaluko* ceremony (isiXhosa)
ilobolo	bride price
indoda	a circumcised man, after *ulwaluko* (isiXhosa)
inkwenkwe	an uncircumcised boy (isiXhosa)
isishumani	shoemaker, colloquial for someone without a sexual partner, or with only one sexual partner over a long period of time (isiXhosa – colloquial)
isisu	damage payment for getting someone pregnant without being married to her. *Ukubhatala isisu* – 'to pay for breaking the stomach' (isiXhosa).
isoka	a Zulu man with multiple sexual partners (isiZulu)
jolling	to party, also used to mean 'having an affair' (Afrikaans – colloquial)
lekka	nice (Afrikaans – colloquial)
loxion	colloquial for township, from the Afrikaans word *lokasie* (location)
mophato	group of men who attended initiation school together and who now constitute an age regiment. Intended as a peer group for mutual advice and support amongst men (pl. *mephato* – seSotho).
mos	like (Afrikaans)
naai	no (Afrikaans – colloquial)
neh	interlocutory, asking a question, 'you understand?' (Afrikaans – colloquial)
ou papa	forward, wanting to know things beyond your age
pleya	a guy who has a lot of women at the same time (isiXhosa – colloquial)
shebeen	small tavern, informal, often unlicensed
skell	scold, complain or moan (Afrikaans)
somma	just (Afrikaans – colloquial)
takkies	trainers, running shoes
tata	father, often a term of respect for a non-relative (isiXhosa)
tik	crystal meth, illegal substance, active ingredient methamphetamine plus various commonly available household substances (Afrikaans)
ukudliwa	the fine payable for transgressing the tribal code of respect (isiXhosa)
ulwaluko	the initiation ceremony for Xhosa boys at around age 18, a requirement for entry into manhood, involves penile circumcision and a period of solitude in the bush (isiXhosa)
umnumzana	a household head (isiZulu)
undize	the children's game of hide and seek (isiXhosa)

1

STUDYING YOUNG FATHERS IN IMPOVERISHED COMMUNITIES

CHAPTER 1

What we know and need to know about young fathers and fatherhood

Over the past two decades there has been a growing focus on teenage or adolescent fathers, many reports of which begin with these or similar words: 'research into adolescent parenting involvement has focused primarily on mothers while neglecting fathers' (Miller 1997: 69; see also Anthony & Smith 1994; Barret & Robinson 1981, 1982; Fry & Trifiletti 1983; Lesser et al. 2001). Where studies do focus on young fathers they tend to be of three types. The first documents young fathers' participation from the *perspective of the mother* rather than of the young father (see, for example, Futris & Schoppe-Sullivan 2007). The second focuses on the nature of young fathers' *own experience of being fathered* in relation to how they participate in parenting their children (Allen & Doherty 1996; Broadfield 2006; Bucklin 1999; Veneziano & Rohner 1998). The third, and by far the majority of studies, investigates the links between early fatherhood and *negative* life outcomes.

Young fatherhood and negative life outcomes

The current literature highlights a litany of negative life outcomes faced by young fathers, such as increased poverty and dependence on welfare expenditure (Giddens & Birdsall 2001; Hardy & Duggan 1988; Mollborn 2006; O'Connor 1998); delinquency and repeat offending by young fathers (Breslin 1998; Florsheim et al. 1999; Resnick et al. 1993; Wei et al. 2002); lower levels of educational attainment (Marsiglio 1986); subsequent diminished employment opportunities and performance in the workplace (Bunting & McAuley 2004; ESRC 1997; O'Connor 1998; Pirog-Good 1996); and poorer health, educational and behavioural outcomes for children born to teenage parents (Thornberry et al. 1997). With regard to employment, the UK's study *Twenty-something in the 1990s: Getting On, Getting By, Getting Nowhere* (ESRC 1997) is of special interest since it investigated, among other things, the level of employment of young men who had become parents while in their teens. It found that by the age of 26, a quarter of young fathers were unemployed and only 4 per cent had professional or managerial jobs compared to 25 per cent of young men who had become fathers in their twenties. The same study also found that 'a quarter of the female respondents who had become mothers while still in their teens were raising their children as *lone parents* by the age of twenty-six' (cited in Giddens & Birdsall 2001: 324, emphasis added).

However, as informative as these studies are, they also point to a dearth of studies that deal with the experience or phenomenon of young fatherhood itself. Where these studies do exist, they, as with the studies previously cited that look at negative employment or delinquency outcomes, also focus on the negative experiences of young fathers. For example, a study by Cruzat and Aracena (2006: 16) highlights the 'disorientation and helplessness' experienced by young fathers; Elster and Hendricks

(1986) focus on the *stresses* of young fatherhood; Dearden et al. (1995: 551) discuss the 'aggressive, truant and law-breaking behaviours' of young men who became fathers in their teen years; and Coleman and Dennison (1998: 12) describe the negative stereotypes propagated by politicians who call young parents 'scroungers on the state'. In contrast, Rhoden and Robinson (1997) and Glikman (2004) provide examples of the very limited number of studies that describe the wider phenomenon of youthful fathering, including the social connections that young fathers need. Rhoden and Robinson's (1997: 105) study shows how 'societal support can cushion the harsh blow for teen dads with positive implications for father, mother, and child'. Glikman's study, on the other hand, interviewed 25 US low-income fathers twice – a year apart – and asked about their experience of fathering in relation to their sense of self. Glikman (2004: 195, 202) reports that 'the majority of young fathers were found to be involved significantly in the lives of their children, despite their own struggles. This in turn helped them feel positive about their sense of self'; and 'young fathers described selves that felt more accomplished, more defined, more complete' after a year of involvement in parenting. Glikman (among others, such as Bunting & McAuley 2004; Hollander 1996; Miller 1997) also provides evidence that refutes contemporary media stereotypes and many quantitative studies,[1] showing that the large majority of young fathers are involved in the care of their children over time.

Despite the paucity of phenomenological studies and the deficit in emphasis of the overall literature on young fathers, it does provide a basic understanding of young fatherhood. We know, for example, that young men who are aggressive as children (Miller-Johnson et al. 2004), who were born to teenage mothers, who do poorly at school, and who begin alcohol use and sexual activity at a young age (Pears et al. 2005) are more likely to father children at a young age. We also know that adolescent or teenage fathers seldom plan to become fathers. Their children arrive as a consequence of sexual activity engaged in impulsively and/or without the use of contraceptives or through contraceptive failure (Miller 1997). While many reports indicate that young fathers' response to fatherhood is denial or escape, we know that, barring a few exceptions – for example, drug addiction and criminal involvement (Jaffee et al. in Morrell 2006) – children benefit from the presence of a caring and supportive father if they are to develop optimally and survive financially (Pruett 1993). At the same time, we also know that young men's expectations, attitudes and approaches to fatherhood are influenced by social exclusion, the availability of sex education, the presence of role models, poverty and cultural expectations as well as 'by media portrayals of sexual conquest and "macho" behaviour' (Giddens & Birdsall 2001: 324).

The absence of studies on young fathers in the developing world

Perhaps the most noteworthy absence in the current literature on young fatherhood is that the existing studies are almost exclusively situated in the global north (see for example Marsiglio 1994; Reeves 2007; Robinson 1988). Consequently, very little is known about the phenomenon of young fatherhood in contexts of pervasive and chronic poverty. Arguably, since many studies focus on *impoverished* British and North American (especially African American) inner-city youth (Allen & Doherty 1996; Anderson 1993a; Davies et al. 2004; McAdoo 1990), there ought to be a number of transferable insights for impoverished young fathers in developing world contexts. And certainly, while issues such as unemployment, absentee fathers (Colman 1993; Lerman 1986; Posel & Devey 2006) and criminal involvement are shared among these young men (and young fathers) in both the global north and the developing world context, it may be argued that the contexts and circumstances of young fathers

---

1   Bunting and McAuley (2004) argue that quantitative studies usually collect data from official court, clinic or hospital records and as such are unable to capture the lived experience of everyday fathering – much of which occurs informally and off the official record.

in the developing world are both more dire and more complex than those of their global north counterparts.

In the developing world, not only do young fathers experience higher levels of poverty and unemployment than those in the global north, but they are also important target groups for HIV prevention and sex education, since HIV infection levels are of greater magnitude in developing world contexts and these young men are clearly sexually active. While many authors in the global north decry the 'invisibility' (Bunting & McAuley 2004; Coleman & Dennison 1998; Reeves 2007) of young fathers, since teenage mothers seldom give the name or age of their partner at birth and the large majority are unaccompanied by the fathers of their children for hospital or clinic visits,[2] such invisibility is exacerbated by the lack of services for young fathers in the developing world. Such compounded invisibility results in making young fathers in the developing world inaccessible for recruitment into sexual health and well-being programmes, which inevitably results in them also slipping through the net for successful HIV interventions.

In the African context, while no recent studies on young fathers exist, there has been a renewed interest in fatherhood in general. In the ground-breaking collection *Baba* (Richter & Morrell 2006), contributors focus attention on a number of issues that are cogent to a study on young fathers. Posel and Devey (2006) portray the extent of absentee fathers,[3] especially among 'black' South African households, while Ramphele and Richter (2006), Wilson (2006) and Hunter (2006) provide some of the arguments for why this might be so. Wilson (2006) and Ramphele and Richter (2006) describe how migrating for labour, since the advent of colonisation and throughout apartheid, has become an entrenched way of life for many 'black' fathers, and is complicit in father absence. In addition, Wilson notes that poverty, including the inability to feed their children, is frequently associated with depression in parents, which lowers their ability to fulfil their parental roles. Furthermore, Hunter writes compellingly about Zulu men's changed traditional roles and socio-economic circumstances, which have robbed them of *amandla* (power) and resulted in their inability to form a household – complicated by (expensive) cultural rituals and expectations, themes taken up by Lesejane (2006)[4] and Mkhize (2006).[5]

So while *Baba* deals with fatherhood in general, many of the issues it raises shed light on the lives of impoverished young fathers, whose experience of fatherhood in the developing world is further compounded by cultural practices and expectations, a universally poor quality of education and information about reproductive health, and complex social relationships in an environment devoid of the social capital (Fagan et al. 2007) taken for granted in middle-class contexts. This study, therefore, aims to begin the conversation of what it means to be poor, young and a father in a developing world context. It is informed by the existing emphases and gaps described in this chapter and is motivated to understand how teenagers living in impoverished communities *experience* fatherhood, the conditions and reasons surrounding their entry into fatherhood, and the ways in which these circumstances – personal, social and environmental – *help or hinder* their subsequent involvement in parenting their children. This monograph aims to contribute such a perspective, from young men and from the key people with whom they are involved.

2   Of course, the partners of many teenage mothers are older men rather than only adolescents. See, for example, Breslin (1997, 1998) and Males and Chew (1996).
3   Posel and Devey (2006: 47) estimate that among 'black' households 63 per cent of fathers are 'disappeared' (12.8 per cent dead, 50.2 per cent absent). This is in contrast to 13.3 per cent disappeared 'white' fathers (2.4 per cent dead and 10.9 per cent absent).
4   Lesejane (2006) describes the traditional roles of a father in Sotho culture as moral custodian, provider, protector, role model to young men and responsible leader; the support systems of initiation for boys; age regiments (*mephato*) for initiates; an inheritance (usually of land) to ensure a young man's ability to provide for a family; and a community dispute forum – most of which has disappeared in contemporary urban living.
5   Mkhize (2006) calls attention to the difficulty young men have in raising *ilobolo* (bride price), arguably due to its commercialisation as well as to the class barriers that cause parents to prohibit marriage for their children.

The purpose of the study

In order to provide such an in-depth portrait of the experiences of impoverished young fathers, this study set out to answer two closely related research questions: (1) How do young men living in poverty, and those involved with them, experience fatherhood? (2) What are the factors that help or hinder young men's engagement in the parenting of their children?

The study was designed to elicit preliminary data that will help define appropriate interventions for young fathers, especially those living in environments of chronic and pervasive poverty. It aims to document and analyse young men's experiences, from finding out about their impending fatherhood to recording the changing nature of their relationships with partners, parents, school and community – in other words, with the members of their existing and newly extended social networks (Anderson 1993a). In hearing and analysing young fathers' stories, special care was taken to distinguish the various ways in which they engage with their children, and to ask how patterns of engagement varied depending on the level of family and community support young fathers received, as well as whether their educational levels and employment status contributed in any way to their parental engagement. Particular care was also taken to document examples of programmatic interventions, where young men have experienced these. Before these data are presented, the following chapter outlines the methodological and ethical strategies employed in undertaking this study.

CHAPTER 2

Designing and implementing an ethical phenomenological study

In order to obtain an ethical and contextual understanding of the phenomenon of young fatherhood in impoverished communities, a number of criteria had to be met in keeping with emancipatory, rights-based, democratic research (Baker et al. 2004; Lynch 1999). First, the conceptual framework needed to allow space for young fathers to express themselves sufficiently and in a way that aided their own recognition of what they might do about their own circumstances. Second, the study needed to be sensitive, with sufficient care being taken to help young men process what for many of them might be difficult disclosures. Third, young men needed to be able to control the research in some aspects, albeit limited, so that their voices were not unnecessarily mediated. In planning the methodology adopted for the study, we sought to fulfil each of these criteria.

The conceptual and methodological framework

The study employed a qualitative, voice-centred and interpretivist approach that used semi-structured phenomenological interviewing (Moustakas 1994) so that young fathers had an opportunity to 'perform…themselves as they are, as they wish they might be, and as they think others imagine them to be' (Luttrell 2003: 150). It allowed them multiple opportunities to speak, reflect and question research findings, their environment and their own experiences – and in so doing offered them some control over the study. Central to the study was an attempt to work from within an ecological framework (Bronfenbrenner 1986, 1992) in which the relationships between the internal family functioning and external systems of young fathers were highlighted, along with social and cultural influences, the role of fathers in their communities, and barriers to fathers' involvement (McAdoo 1993). Through careful interviewing as well as by mapping social networks (Freeman et al. 1989; Friemel 2007; Purvez 2003), these goals were set and achieved for the study. So while young fathers' experiences, emotions, perceptions, understandings and interpretations of their roles as fathers were central to this study, their immediate social relationships[6] (parents, siblings, partners, friends and community) and cultural and religious[7] contexts also formed an important part of this investigation.

Social networks proved to be an important theoretical framework through which to view young fatherhood, since teenage young men have limited power to make autonomous choices. Not only were

---

6   In keeping with the conventional wisdom that it takes a village to raise a child.
7   Cultural contexts emerged as being of greater importance than religious contexts, with young men speaking very little of the significance of religion in their lives or in the circumstances surrounding the birth of their child. Only young Muslim 'coloured' men who had fathered a child with a Christian partner spoke of the significance of religion.

these young men less capable of making mature decisions by virtue of their ages, they were often pre-vented from doing so by their parents or by the parents of the mother of their child (MOC). Members of social networks interviewed by young fathers, including but not limited to their parents, provided insightful data on how these young men responded to the news of their impending fatherhood, what steps they took (or failed to take) to prepare themselves for parenthood, and how their relationship with their child developed in the ensuing months and years.

Data were therefore analysed through a social–ecological framework and also took account of vari-ables such as the age of the young men when they became fathers and their ages at the time of the study to provide insight into the effect of the passage of time; the level of young men's education and how or whether fathering interrupted their education; whether they were currently employed; their experiences of sex education; the components of their family unit at the time of the study; as well as their familial, social, cultural and religious affiliations, i.e. whether they had completed religious cer-emonies such as baptism, or cultural rituals such as *ulwaluko* (initiation), or damage payments (*isisu*). Pathways of being uninvolved, involved and partially involved from the beginning of their fatherhood to date were also explored, along with their understandings of masculinity and of parenting itself.

Data collection, research sample and analysis

The study proceeded in three phases. The first phase comprised a series of two semi-structured indi-vidual interviews with a sample of 27 'black' and 'coloured' young fathers living in contexts of poverty in the Western Cape and KwaZulu-Natal (for a total of 52 interviews).[8] Appendix 1 details the interview schedules that were used in interviews and shows how questions were designed to be open-ended, to elicit narratives as well as to provide opportunities for reflection and data triangulation over the course of the study. Included in the two interviews were two interactive activities. The first, called a 'four field map' by Sturgess et al. (2001), presented young fathers with, in this case, three rather than four concentric circles, each smaller than the next and placed inside each other. Young fathers were then tasked to write down in any of the circles the names or designations of the people involved in the story of them and their baby, representing the closeness of the relationship. Figure 2.1 provides a sample of a completed 'three field map'.

The second interactive component of the interviews asked young men to list, in order of priority, the three things or people that helped them to be a good father and the three things or people that hin-dered them from being a good father (see Figure 2.2).

For the second phase of the study, a number of young men were invited to participate further by ask-ing approximately eight members of their social networks (e.g. MOC, father, mother, sibling, teacher, friend, MOC's mother, MOC's father, MOC's friend, community leader, nurse, minister, traditional healer, youth leader or grandparent) to participate in a short interview. While young men were keen to participate, the time of the year (October) and closeness to exams was a hindrance for many. In addition, many young men expressed fear at having to speak to the parents of the mother of their child. Ultimately, only four young men agreed to and were able to complete the assignment. Two interviewed social network members using a digital voice recorder, while the other two took notes and then wrote up responses immediately afterwards. The recording medium seemed to have little impact on the quality of data produced.

---

8   Two young men were not available for second interviews. Ntombisa had returned to the Eastern Cape after being unable to find work in Cape Town, and Bongani was writing matric exams when the researcher was in Durban to conduct interviews.

FIGURE 2.1   *A 'three field map' depicting people involved in a young father's life*

Source: Onathi, 20, Langa, Western Cape

FIGURE 2.2   *A 'most helpful, least helpful' priority list*

People/things	MOST helpful	People/Things	LEAST helpful
My mom My uncle		Not working	
	1		1
People/things	MOST helpful	People/Things	LEAST helpful
My sister		Not Living with them	
	2		2
People/things	MOST helpful	People/Things	LEAST helpful
My Father		To not having relationship with her mom	
	3		3

Source: Tapelo, 23, Khayelitsha, Western Cape

Although it was originally envisaged that researchers themselves might conduct these interviews, it soon became apparent that this would not be a sensitive or respectful way to proceed, since for many young fathers these relationships were still fraught. Similarly, an initial idea to video-record interviews was also rejected for the same reasons. Both decisions were taken in consultation with the young fathers who had agreed to participate in the study. In the event, the interviews *conducted by the young fathers* were extremely well executed and provided rich data and displayed potential as a model for intervention. The four young men involved in social network interviews conducted a total of 25 interviews between them. Appendix 1 also provides sample questions for this group of people. Counted together, the first two phases of the study produced 77 interviews in total from young fathers and their social networks in Cape Town and Durban. The third phase of the study comprised an afternoon debrief and consultation workshop in which young fathers who participated in the study were invited to discuss the findings and clarify, question or propose alternative explanations. This phase will be more fully elucidated when the issue of research ethics is discussed.

Choosing a study sample

The extent of teenage fertility in South Africa has been measured at various intervals and ranges from 78 births per 1 000 young women between 15 and 19 in 1996, to an estimated 65 per 1 000 in 2001, and 73 per 1 000 in 2005 (Moultrie & McGrath 2007: 442). However, what is most interesting to note, and has guided this study, is the different rates of teenage fertility among each of the so-called population groups in South Africa. In 1998 the South African Demographic and Health Survey (DoH 2002) revealed that fertility rates for 'black' and 'coloured' female teenagers were four times as high as those for 'white' and 'Indian' teenagers. Based on the 2001 census, Moultrie and Dorrington (2004) estimate that the ratio of 'black' teenage fertility has increased from 4.0 to 5.5 times as high as fertility among 'white' teenagers, and among 'coloured' teens from 4.0 to 4.5 times as high as among 'white' teens. These statistics were the primary drivers in focusing this study on 'black' and 'coloured' teenage fathers. In addition, rates of teen fertility (along with HIV infection)[9] in informal settlements are significantly higher than in other communities (Shisana et al. 2005; Simbayi et al. 2004). Therefore, since 'the incidence of teen pregnancy is inversely linked to socio-economic [status]',[10] and the purpose of this study was to identify the experiences of impoverished young men who become fathers during their teenage years, research participants were 'black' and 'coloured' young men recruited from peri-urban townships, informal settlements and student communities in the Western Cape and KwaZulu-Natal.[11] In both the Western Cape and KwaZulu-Natal, people living in townships and informal settlements tend to regularly migrate between rural and peri-urban areas for holidays, funerals, and cultural and other family events and so the sample was carefully selected to include young fathers who had recently migrated from the rural areas. A group of young 'coloured' men from the previously 'coloured' area of Bonteheuwel in Cape Town was also included to compare 'black' and 'coloured' fathers' experiences. In KwaZulu-Natal, research participants were recruited from Bonella and Cato Manor townships, the surrounding informal settlements, and from among the student population adjoining Mayville.

For two main reasons, research participants were recruited (through a variety of means – see later) from among 'black' and 'coloured' young men living in contexts of poverty (where poverty was defined

---

9   HIV infection among 'black' youth aged 15–24 (12.3 per cent) is seven times as high as infection rates among 'coloured' youth (1.7 per cent), 41 times as high as among 'white' youth (0.3 per cent) and 15 times as high as among Indian youth (0.8 per cent) (Shisana et al. 2005: 38).

10 Harrison (2008, citing Sibanda 2004: 99) also makes the connection between socio-economic status, school dropouts and teen pregnancy. Poor young people (especially young women) who drop out of school are more likely to become pregnant than their peers who remain in school.

11 Teen fertility rates in KwaZulu-Natal and the Western Cape were representative of national figures. In addition, KwaZulu-Natal (16.1 per cent) has the highest rate of HIV infection among youth aged between 15 and 24 while the Western Cape (2.3 per cent) has the lowest infection rates (Shisana et al. 2005: 37).

by a R593 minimum living level per capita).[12] First, 'black' youth make up nearly 80 per cent of South Africa's youth population and so capturing their experience is most representative of South Africa's population demographic. Second, young men who father children during adolescence and who are living in poverty are more exposed to negative life outcomes than their middle-class peers. That is not to say that the experiences of young men who are 'Indian' or 'white' are any less important; however, this study is focused on how *poverty* influences young fatherhood, and by far the largest proportion of people living in poverty in South Africa are 'black' (Armstrong et al. 2008; Terreblanche 2002).

The danger in only including young 'black' and 'coloured' youth in the study, however, lies in the fact that some may interpret the findings along narrow 'racial' stereotypes. However, if these findings are to be used to inform interventions among impoverished youth, not only in South Africa but also in other parts of sub-Saharan Africa, then it is an unavoidable fact that it is 'black' and 'coloured' youth who are mainly impoverished, and that the sample as contained in this study will therefore have greater potential for transferable insights.

A number of reasons informed the choice to focus on young men who were aged between 14 and 20 at the time they became fathers. First, becoming a father before 14 is a rare occurrence and access to these young men is limited, whereas the phenomenon is not unusual among young men between the ages of 14 and 20. Second, existing literature suggests that young men between the ages of 14 and 20 who become fathers seem to be most negatively affected by fatherhood, since it jeopardises educational outcomes, job opportunities and participation in present and future fathering (ESRC 1997).

Tables 2.1 and 2.2 (pages 13–16) provide comprehensive details about the sample of young fathers who participated in the study and include data about geographical location, level of education, age, family relationships, employment status, the reason for becoming a young father, their age at the time of becoming a young father and at the time of the study, as well as the ages of their child and the mother of their child. All names used in the demographic tables and throughout this report are pseudonyms chosen by the young fathers themselves. In places where they identify members of their family by name, these have been anonymised. While the youngest participant in the study was 17 and the oldest 24, the youngest age at which a participant became a father was 14 and the oldest 20. Both the average and the median age for research participants was 20 and the average and the median age at which they became fathers was 17.

Due to the small sample size and qualitative nature of this study, findings are not statistically representative and therefore not generalisable. However, it is clear from the demographics (provided in Tables 2.1 and 2.2) that the young fathers who participated in the study are indicative of the diversity of impoverished young men in South Africa, and therefore this study can be used in making transferable insights (Maxwell 1996).

Analysing the data

Data were recorded and transcribed verbatim and then open-coded using a qualitative data analysis package (Atlas.ti) before a more analytical coding, using narrative readings and thematic coding, was performed.

---

12 While participants were not paid for their participation, they were provided with R100 for each interview (R50 for social network interviews) in which they participated in order to cover transport and meal costs for the day, irrespective of where the interview was held. In some cases interviews involved the research participant travelling to a mutually agreed upon venue (usually one of the HSRC offices), while in others the researcher travelled to the young man's place of residence or school.

Using community informants to recruit research participants

The sample was sourced using community informants and so overcame one of the largest problems cited in research and intervention among young fathers – that of 'invisibility' (Bunting & McAuley 2004; Coleman & Dennison 1998; Reeves 2007), i.e. the difficulty of locating young fathers. Community informants had a history of involvement in research studies with both authors, and were paid for travel and food expenses whilst they were recruiting. The criterion they were given was simply to find young men who lived in the chosen communities (informal settlements, townships and, in the case of Bonteheuwel, a poor 'coloured' community). The notion and definition of impoverishment was discussed with community informants. Instead of asking potential participants to explicitly state their income, where participants lived and whether or where they worked were considered to be good indications of a minimum living level of under R600 per capita, as required by our definition.

Making use of community informants turned out to be a productive means of accessing these 'invisible' young men, and provided interesting data on who constitutes the best kind of recruiter for such a study (and potentially for outreach work among young fathers). In Langa in the Western Cape, most informants were similarly aged young men living in the community; they easily identified young fathers from among their peers and introduced them to the researcher. When young women were asked to recruit participants for the study, only one was successful in convincing a young father to participate. On the other hand, when young men were asked to recruit participants, they had more willing candidates than the study could accommodate. In KwaZulu-Natal, the community informant was a local council waste-removal worker. He had a wide network since he regularly spent time in the community and had come to know many of the young men, including those who were fathers. In Bonteheuwel in the Western Cape, young fathers were recruited by a middle-aged woman with a history of community involvement through local NGOs. She, too, was successful at recruiting participants, although she took longer to do so than male recruiters. During the consultation workshop with young fathers at the end of the study, they were asked whether using community informants, most of whom were known to them, constituted fair practice in research. The young men replied that it was difficult to say no to these people, whom they knew, even though they might have been reluctant to participate and would probably have said no to a stranger. They concluded that it was not an unfair practice since it was important for their stories to become known and that using community informants provided a catalyst to achieve this end. Others said they agreed to participate because they thought it 'might help me know how to help my child', 'find solutions' and because 'I really just wanted [to] talk to someone about being a young father and I've never had the opportunity to do so before'. What was not explored, however, was these young men's response to being interviewed by women.

Research ethics

The study as a whole was approved by the Human Sciences Research Council's (HSRC's) Research Ethics Committee. In addition to confidentiality and anonymity, the young men, their parents/guardians if under the age of 18, and members of their social networks were asked for active informed consent after having the study carefully explained to them (see Appendix 2), including the benefits and potential discomforts they might experience. In addition, young men were offered referrals to a community, social, youth or mental health worker if needed. Although none took up this offer, it was clear that some young men became distressed during interviews, yet preferred to speak to the researcher rather than a helping professional.

TABLE 2.1   Young fathers research study: Basic demographic data, part 1

Name	Location	Age		Age of child		Mother of child's age		Exclusive	Relationship with MOC*		Relationship with child
		then	now	then	now	then	now		then	now	
'Coloured' young men, Cape Town											
Fadiel[a]	Bonteheuwel	17 and 17	19		2 and 2	16 and 16	18 and 18	No	Together with one of MOC		Both regular
Ibrahiem	Bonteheuwel	18	20		2	16	18	Yes	Together		Regular
Marlin[b]	Bonteheuwel	14 and 15	18		3 and 4	15 and 17	19	Yes	Together		Regular
Sabier	Bonteheuwel	17	18		1	16	17	Yes	Together		Regular
Yusuf	Bonteheuwel	16	21		5	20	25	No	Together	Not together – acrimonious	Furtive
Zaid	Bonteheuwel	17	18		1	17	18	Yes	Together		Regular
IsiXhosa young men, Cape Town											
Andile	Langa	20	21		1	17	18	Yes	Together		Regular
Jabu	Khayelitsha / Joe Slovo (Inf.)**	18	22		4	Doesn't know		No	Not together		Regular – GS***
Lonwabo	Langa	18	24		6	25	31	No	Not together		Furtive
Luthando[c]	Langa	18 and 19	21		Miscarried; 2	17	19	Yes	Together		Regular
Luxolo	Langa	17	20		3	14	17	No	Together	Not together	Occasional – GS
Lwandile	Joe Slovo (Inf.)/ Kyamnandi	15	17		2	17	19	No	Not together		Furtive
Lwethu[d]	Langa	17 and 18	19		Miscarried; 1	19 and 20	21	No	Not together		Regular

Name	Location	Age		Age of child	Mother of child's age		Exclusive	Relationship with MOC*		Relationship with child
		then	now	now	then	now		then	now	
Ntombisa	Langa/Mthatha	16	18	2	15	17	No	Not together		Occasional – GS
Onathi	Langa	20	20	<1	16	16	Yes	Together		Regular
Saki	Bellville/Mthatha	18	24	6	16	22	Yes/No	Together	Not together	Regular – GS
Siya	Aliwal North/Langa	14	17	4	17	21	No/Yes	Not together	Together	Regular – GS
Tapelo	Khayelitsha	17	23	6	15	21	No	Not together		Regular
Vuyo	Langa	15	17	2	15	17	No	Together	Not together	Regular
Xolile	Khayelitsha	17	24	7	18	25	No	Together		Regular
isiZulu young men, Durban										
Bongani	Mayville	17	18	1	18	19	No	Together	Not together	Occasional – GS
Dumisani	Mayville	19	20	1	18	19	No	Not together		Occasional – GS
Lungile	Cato Crest (Inf.)	18	23	5	16	21	No	Together		Occasional – GS
Nhlanhla[b]	Bonella	18 and 21	21	3 and <1	18	20	No	Not together	Together	Regular
Sakhile	Mayville	17	19	2	18	20	No	Together		Occasional – GS
S'bu	Mayville	17	18	1	15	16	Yes	Together		Regular – GS
Sifiso	Bonella	18	23	5	17	22	No	Not together		Occasional – GS

Notes: *MOC = mother of child

**Inf. = Informal settlement

***GS = geographically separated

a Fadiel has two children, each with a different woman.

b Marlin and Nhlanhla each have two children with their respective partners.

c & d Both Luthando's and Lwethu's two impregnations were with the same young woman.

TABLE 2.2 Young fathers research study: Basic demographic data, part 2

Name	Employment status	Education	Relationship with own father	Child's surname	Child's caregiver	Reason for pregnancy	Services or programmes
'Coloured' young men, Cape Town							
Fadiel	Unemployed	Grade 10 (dropped)	Sporadic/Mother deceased	Mother's	MOC*	No condoms	None
Ibrahiem	Unemployed	Grade 9 (dropped)	Absent – deceased	Mother's	YF** and his mother/MOC	Burst condom	None
Marlin	Unemployed	Grade 9 (dropped)	Present	Mother's	MOC – lives with his parents	No condoms	None
Sabier	Unemployed	Grade 10 (expelled)	Present	Mother's	MOC & her parents/YF & his parents	Wanted a child	None
Yusuf	Employed	Grade 10 (dropped)	Present	Mother's	MOC's mother	No condoms	None
Zaid	Employed	Grade 12	Absent – no contact	Mother's	MOC	No condoms	None
IsiXhosa young men, Cape Town							
Andile	Schooling/Casual work	Grade 10 (in school)	Present	Mother's	MOC & MOC's mother	Wanted a child	None
Jabu	Schooling	Grade 11 (in school)	Absent – little contact	Mother's/father's	YF's sister	Alcohol	None
Lonwabo	Unemployed/Casual work	Grade 9 (dropped)	Absent – no contact	Mother's	MOC & MOC's parents	Alcohol	None
Luthando	Employed	Grade 12 (failed)	Absent – little contact	Mother's	MOC & MOC's mother	Girl lied about contraception/No condoms	None
Luxolo	Employed	Grade 12	Present	Mother's	MOC	No condoms	None
Lwandile	Schooling	Grade 11 (in school)	Absent – no contact/mother deceased	Father's	MOC & MOC's mother	No condoms	PPASA*** Peer Education
Lwethu	Unemployed	Grade 12	Absent – regular contact	Mother's	MOC & MOC's mother	No condoms	loveLife Positive Sexuality

Name	Employment status	Education	Relationship with own father	Child's surname	Child's caregiver	Reason for pregnancy	Services or programmes
Ntombisa	Unemployed	Grade 9 (dropped)	Absent – deceased	Mother's	MOC & MOC's mother	Game – hide and seek	None
Onathi	Schooling/College	Grade 12 (in school)	Present/Father shot	Mother's	MOC & MOC's mother	No condoms	None
Saki	Studying	Grade 12	Present	Mother's	YF's parents	No condoms	Social worker
Siya	Schooling/Casual work	Grade 11 (in school)	Absent/Present	Father's	MOC's parents	No condoms	Baptist Church
Tapelo	Casual work/Unemployed	Grade 9 (dropped)	Present/Mother deceased	Mother's	Mother	No condoms	None
Vuyo	Schooling	Grade 10 (in school)	Absent – no contact	Mother's	MOC & MOC's mother	No condoms	None
Xolile	Unemployed	Grade 9 (dropped)	Present/Separated	Father's	Mother	No condoms	Men's clinic at rank

IsiZulu young men, Durban

Name	Employment status	Education	Relationship with own father	Child's surname	Child's caregiver	Reason for pregnancy	Services or programmes
Bongani	Schooling	Grade 12 (in school)	Absent – no contact	Mother's	MOC	Burst condom	None
Dumisani	Studying	Grade 12	Absent – regular contact	Mother's	MOC & MOC's mother	Bad luck	None
Lungile	Unemployed	Grade 9 (dropped)	Absent – deceased	Mother's	MOC's aunt	Mistake	None
Nhlanhla	Self-employed	Grade 12	Present	Mother's	MOC	Alcohol	None
Sakhile	Studying	Grade 12	Present	Father's	YF's mother	Wanted a child	None
S'bu	Unemployed	Grade 12 (failed)	Present	Father's	YF's mother/MOC's mother	No condoms	None
Sifiso	Studying	Grade 12	Absent – no contact	Mother's	MOC's mother	No condoms	None

Notes: *MOC = mother of child
    **YF = young father
    ***PPASA = Planned Parenthood Association of South Africa

Debriefing and consultation workshop

A lengthy debriefing and consultation workshop was conducted in Cape Town[13] after a draft report had been produced, and was attended by most Cape Town-based research participants. A few participants were unable to attend due to clashes with work. This constituted phase three of the study and served three purposes. The first was to allow the young men to meet with the possibility of forming informal peer networks, which might serve to help them in their roles as young fathers. Second, it allowed researchers to address any feelings of distress that may have arisen in a supportive environment. Gathering participants together for a meeting allowed researchers to make a further offer of help and referral to these young men. Third, and most crucially in keeping with the spirit of democratic and rights-based research, the young men were offered an opportunity to tell researchers 'what you think about what we've said about what you said'. And this they did in torrents over pizza and Coke one cloudy summer's afternoon in the 'chill area' of the HSRC offices in Cape Town.

The debriefing and consultation workshop provided a number of important insights. Of course, it fulfilled the technical criteria of reliability and participation that the study had set out to achieve through 'member checks' (Maxwell 1996), but it also revealed much more. One of the researchers did a brief presentation of each chapter, accompanied by a community informant who had previously read the report, summarised it and translated it into isiXhosa. Where necessary, young men were asked specific questions to begin the conversation, but that soon became unnecessary as they animatedly discussed each chapter, agreed with some of it, questioned parts of it and appeared to be having a great time doing so. Sometimes the discussion merely reinforced aspects of the report, but at other times participants asked for sections to be expanded, or for additions. Most notably, young men commented that Chapter 6, which deals with their lack of condom use and multiple concurrent partnerships (MCPs), did not paint them in a good light, yet they agreed it was an integral part of the report since it highlighted their 'irresponsibility' and 'life as it is in *ikasi* [the township]'. In contrast, they noted how Chapters 3 to 5 spoke of the 'responsible things' they did and 'the struggle and difficult things of our lives' or environment. Where young men suggested changes, amendments or additions, these were considered and have been incorporated into this final report, where pertinent.

Perhaps the most striking aspect of this debriefing and consultation workshop was the stark contrast it represented with a traditional school Life Orientation or sex education session. These young men, who, at their own admission, frequently did not talk in sex education classes or simply fooled around, were engaged in the project, even took ownership and directed the discussion. Those who had conducted social network interviews were asked to tell of their experience in doing so and many others asked if they could also do it now that the school holidays loomed. The workshop and the series of interviews (individual, interactive and with social networks) certainly contained elements of a potential future intervention with so-called invisible young fathers.

Limitations and challenges of the study

The study began in June 2008 and was completed by the end of the same year. Preparation work took two months, including satisfying the strict criteria of the Research Ethics Committee of the HSRC and recruiting participants. Interviews then occurred between August and October, with initial interviews proving more time-consuming than second interviews – many of which were conducted during school holidays. For most young men, there were four to six weeks between interviews. Researchers and community informants worked together to ensure young fathers' participation in the second round of interviews, with a high rate of success (only two young men were unable to attend second interviews).

---

13   Due to time constraints no debriefing and consultation workshop was held in Durban.

Were there more time, the study could have benefited from involving more young men in social network interviews, which would have provided more information for better data verification as well as a stronger indication of its usefulness as an intervention.

The greatest challenge, however, was transcription. Interviews were conducted in English, isiZulu, isiXhosa, Afrikaans or a mixture of languages. For this reason, transcription proved to be difficult and skilled native language speakers had to be sourced and employed. Transcribers had to understand the language young people used, difficult accents, local colloquialisms and, in cases where English was used, frequently poor renditions of it. The time taken to complete transcription was sorely underestimated and needs to be better planned for in future studies of this nature.

The largest limitation of the study, and one that was expected, was that those young fathers who deny paternity were not recruited into this study since they were largely unidentifiable, and seldom agreed to participate in the cases where it was possible to identify them. This may lead to an assumption that all young fathers are as engaged in the fathering of their children, or at least as troubled by their own struggles, as the young men in this study appear to be. This is, of course, clearly not the case. To the extent, however, that this study reflects upon a little-known discourse of young fathers' struggles and attempts to be involved in the lives of their children, it provides a fresh voice in the phenomenon of being a young father in an impoverished community.

2

**THE VOICES OF
YOUNG FATHERS**

CHAPTER 3

'Scared, proud, excited, frustrated, stressed': Coming to terms with being a young father

'Tell me a little about yourself and the circumstances surrounding when you became a father' – this was the opening invitation 27 nervous young fathers were given as they sat opposite a researcher, having previously agreed to participate in this study. None hesitated. They cleared their throats, put their cellphones on silent and launched into a 10-minute monologue. And while the opening question was constructed to allow young fathers to build their own narratives of fatherhood, it was the sheer force of the strong emotions which accompanied their stories that left a lasting impression, sometimes even days after interviews had been conducted. Responses to hearing the news of the pregnancy, feelings about being a father, the fear with which they disclosed to parents, stories about their children, thinking about how they wanted to be remembered by their child and what made them good (or bad) fathers – in fact, nearly every question asked elicited strong emotions. These young men were honest and passionate about being fathers. Most spoke at length of their shock, fear and disbelief upon hearing the news that they had impregnated someone:

Onathi: I was scared of – I was shocked…And I told Tee [my girlfriend], 'Don't tell my parents'…I was scared, because my mother and father spent a lot – a lot of money on me…I was scared, well, what will they think [about] this new problem…I was embarrassed, because I know Tee was still young, 16. So, I was embarrassed, like, what the family would take me for, or all that stuff…I was so scared. I told my mother…then she was shocked…Then, there was an argument, and it was stressing me like – it was stressing…My father said, 'Boy, you're on your own. I'm not getting into that. I told you that you must use a condom. And why you didn't use it?' I say, 'No man, it was a mistake, man. I didn't mean it to happen'…It did give me quite a stress. I was stressing big time…It was stressing me. My marks did go a little lower, but I told myself I have to pass, so I did. But – Tee being pregnant did stress me a lot. [I was worried about] who's gonna pay – who's gonna pay for the baby? Who's gonna support the baby? All those questions. I keep asking myself all those questions.

Luthando: It was a hell of a frustration, because I'm still at school and then she was still young…She was 17 years…so I thought that, heh, it will be embarrassment to other people, because this is not nice…[We went to the clinic] – there she was told that she was pregnant. I decided to pretend like [I was] her brother, because I'm looking younger than her. [When we got home] I told nobody – until the – baby was showing. I was just afraid…of the parents of course, her parents. And I was just worried, when it comes to my family – because my mother was struggling.

The biggest fear young men had was disappointing their parents, followed almost immediately by how they were going to care for the child:

Tapelo: When I became a father I was about, uh, I think 17/18, so. It was like, uh, at that time I heard that I was going to be a father, it was a bad time for me. That's why I didn't know what I could do, and uh, how – what I'm going to do to support the child.

Luxolo: Yah, it was terrible – I was 17, my girlfriend was still young [14], because she was born on June 1991, you see? So when she told me she's pregnant, I didn't believe it, because I didn't think I can have a child now…I didn't want to hear it, you see?…I'm ashamed, you see? So, I can't tell my parents…So for three months I just ignored my child and her mother. And if I saw them coming in front, I just take another way. Because I don't want to see them… You see. I felt – eeehhh – I don't know how I can explain. Where will I get the money, you see – [I was] stressing – [about how] to support the child.

Ibrahiem: It was a big shock. But a baby is a wonderful thing. I don't feel like a real father because I'm not working. I'm not supporting and that. A father's job is to support his family and I'm not doing that and that's what makes me feel a bit down.

Many young men spoke of the length of time it took them to tell their mothers or parents.

Dumisani: It took me two weeks to tell someone. I was stressed; I didn't know how I was going to do it. But at the end I had to tell my mom…I knew it was my child but I didn't know what to do; I didn't accept it.

For a number of young men, the matter was complicated by the fact that they were no longer in a relationship with the mother of their child (e.g. Nhlanhla) or, like Siya, the mother of their child was only one among multiple partners:

Nhlanhla: It was very hard, you know. And I was still at school I remember, and she told me she was pregnant and I was with someone else and yoh! [pause] and I couldn't tell that person that I've impregnated someone.

Siya: The year that I got my girlfriend pregnant was 2004, late 2004, and then what happened was – um, I was ending up in a position whereby I was having many girlfriends. So when she told me that she was pregnant…at that point it was very difficult for her to tell me that I got her pregnant because of my reputation as far as girls was concerned…But it wasn't easy in terms of telling my family…My first response was, 'Are you insane?' or something… So what I said was, 'Ok [pause] what you're telling me now I can't respond to it now. I need some time to think.'

Young men spoke at length about the conflicting emotions they struggled with when hearing about the pregnancy:

Xolile: So I was just confused, how can she be pregnant? She says to me, 'How can you ask me that question, because we didn't even use a condom?' I said, 'No, I am still at school. And I'm scared – I'm scared to tell my parents that'…I was scared. I was too young to have the baby. I was scared for my parents.

Saki described how, in his confusion, he 'asked questions [of his girlfriend] which I was never supposed to ask, like "How did this happen? Do you think that I'm the father?" – such things' – and how that caused a rift in their relationship that was hard to breach. He also described his own experience of losing 'two friends, male friends – for such a thing' – referring to the suicide of two friends who became fathers at an early age because their parents 'throw words at something that is done'.

Zaid told of how he just felt resigned to the fact:

Zaid: I went to go sit next to her [his girlfriend]. Then I was holding her. Told her, 'Bee, we should just face this thing now…you're already over three months, so there's nothing we can do. The only thing we can do is to support each other and tell our mothers. They are gonna *skell* [scold] but will love the child.' And then, yah, she was crying that day also. She was crying, and I was just holding her and then we were talking.

Fadiel, whose mother died when he was 11 and whose father had recently abandoned him in the keep of his older sister, tells of how, at 17, he felt 'a bit nervous' when he heard that he was going to become a father and that he 'started doing for the first one [baby] what a father should do'. It was only two months later, when he heard that he had impregnated his 'other girlfriend' and that the babies were due days apart in September, that 'it was a bit much for me. I was just confused. I wanted to get out of it…I tried not to allow that to get me down. I was confused because I was a bit young…I thought – [pause] I drank a lot, smoked dope. Everything.'

Fear of parents

Young men's fear of their parents was a surprising feature of their stories:

Sifiso: But before I told my mom, I was scared, I didn't know what to do as I was still in school; I didn't know how will I support the child.

Xolile: I was scared. Yah, I was too young to have the baby. I was scared for my parents. Because the fact is my parents are very strict…I didn't even [go] home for two days. I go to sleep at my grandmother…I thought they were going to beat me…[I] stay at my grandmother's for a week. Because when I left my grandmother, I was going to be in big trouble. So, after that, they made the rules. I must come at school and stay at home and do my homework. After my homework, I'm going to church. So, I told myself, 'No, I'm supposed to do this, because if I didn't do this, I'm going to be in big trouble.' They was going to punish me and beat me.

Luxolo: I run away, because I don't want to face my parents. There's this small gate for the cow when going to the kraal, you see? So I jumped the fence in the garden and ran away when her uncles came to see my parents…My father, my mother. They can shout me. They can shout me, and I disappoint them. Because they trusted me very much. Very much.

These young men's fear of their parents was an interesting and complicated phenomenon. Particularly among the young 'black' men, almost all of them spoke of a genuine fear of their parents' response – whether they lived in single-parent households, with extended family (due to the death or absence of parents) or with both parents. When interrogated about why they were so fearful – was it for fear of physical beatings? – they answered a resounding 'no'. It was because of the emotional tirade that the news would launch, which was ultimately a precursor to the fact that there were enormous financial implications for the young father's family. There would be damage payments (*isisu*) for both ama-

Xhosa and amaZulu young men, as well as possibly the added burden of a payment for transgressing the code of *hlonipha* (respect) and having to pay *ukudliwa*[14] and following the traditional practices of negotiations). Lwethu begins the explanation:

Lwethu: It's kind of complicated. You see, it – it goes back on the way you've br-, you've been brought up, you see? If your parents are strict from day one – and they are your providers obviously. So, you are – you – you are forced to be afraid, cos they provide for you. What are – what are you going to say? You live in the same roof. You have to obey the rules of the house, you see? So, that's why you get scared of your parents…You can't read their minds. But you – you – you just get afraid. I don't know how to explain it. You just get afraid.

Dumisani: The stress was for that – my father is over-strict, you see [pause]. He always advised all his children; like having a child it is not something he liked. My dad liked that a person should complete schooling first and have certain things [pause] then one can have a child. I was scared of things like that [pause] and I was thinking [pause] how am I going to face him. He has always said that he doesn't want such things to happen [pause] but I broke his rules and that is what stressed me a lot.

This parent-induced stress was most intriguing. Most of these young men were in their late teens, yet they expressed an enormous fear of the displeasure of their parents, both mothers and fathers alike. Only a very few feared physical violence (like Xolile), and even fewer that they would be 'chased from the house' (like Bongani and Sabier). It would seem that these young men felt a strong sense of shame more in keeping with breaking family and cultural bonds, and with upsetting the foundation of strong mutual respect and trust in the traditional family.

As might be expected, there were young men who were afraid of the MOC's parents, especially her father. Siya described how when he went to see her parents, he 'stood next to the door…I was waiting for anything to happen'. But for the most part, young men frequently went with their partner to speak to her mother, and avoided her father. Lungile tells of how his girlfriend's father 'put her out of the house':

Lungile: Her mother did not have a problem; the person who had a problem was only her father. Because when he heard, he was still working at Empangeni – when he heard the news he came back on a weekend and he chased her at night and the child was still small. She called me at night asking me to come fetch her with the child. I went to fetch her and stayed with her at my family home. After he had left I took her back to her home again. After a short while she told me that her aunt wants her to stay with her. Her mother didn't have a problem. But I know that nobody would be happy if his child is pregnant at a young age.

For many young men, there was no need to fear their MOC's father's response, because the young woman lived in a single-parent household and the single parent (usually a mother) tended to be more understanding than angry. In contrast, not one of the 'coloured' young fathers reported fear of their own parents. For most of them, their mothers and fathers understood, although their sons were quickly admonished to go find a job:

Yusuf: No, they were not angry. They just knocked some sense into me. They told me that I am a man now, so I must find a job because they can't support me and the baby.

14   These will be more fully covered in Chapter 5.

School and education

Besides parents' instructing their sons to find jobs to support their children, young men also displayed strong emotions around having to abandon their education, or having to watch as their partners abandoned theirs. A number of young men stopped school in solidarity with the mother of their child, and spent a year or two working before going back to school. Jabu took two years off before returning to school despite being 'embarrassed, because you see now I was older'. Siya took a year off and worked in a hardware store before returning to school. He says that dropping out of school was the key to forming a good relationship with the mother of his child's family:

Siya: I was very scared…and then I remembered – I said just a few words which were, 'I am prepared to drop out of school for a year'. And that is just what I said. And telling them that I was there for her support…her father told me to come and sit down, and then we talked.

At the time of writing, both Jabu and Siya were completing Grade 11. Jabu was 22 and Siya was 17. Their tenacity is not mirrored in the majority of young fathers. Those who drop out to work to provide for their children seldom make it back into the education system. This was especially true of the young 'coloured' fathers:

Marlin: My mother said I must go look for a job, I must leave school and I must look after my kids. Then I left school and I found myself some casual jobs.

Yusuf: I didn't finish. I dropped out in Grade 10 because the baby came and I had to go and find a job.

All had either dropped out prior to becoming fathers or their impending fatherhood had been the catalyst for them quitting school. Only Zaid returned to a Further Education and Training (FET) college and completed his final school year.

Saki tells of how, when he got his girlfriend pregnant, 'the teachers got involved…they wanted to know, how can she not be going to school whereas I'm going to school? She stopped and then – I also had to stop then. Until my parents went to school, and then they sat and talked until they reached an agreement.' In the end Saki completed his schooling and allowed his parents to raise the child with the mother of his child's permission. In defending his decision, he says that 'if I had quit school then, I may be working as a grass cutter today.' Today Saki is in his second year at Cape Peninsula University of Technology studying entrepreneurship, and his six-year-old son knows him as his brother.

For the most part, young men reported (perhaps overly optimistically) that the mother of their child had returned to school within a year of having had the baby, leaving the child in the care of her mother or extended family (often in rural areas for young 'black' women). Those who did not return to school, young men explained, did not do so because they had alcohol or drug problems.

Positive emotional responses

Not all of the young fathers who participated in this study had negative emotional responses to the news of their impending fatherhood – at least four reported that they were excited or happy:

Sakhile: Instead of being shocked I was very excited [laughs].

Vuyo: I feel good, very good. And I'm proud. So yah, I can't run. I'm proud. I can't run away, because – because she's my child.

Lonwabo: I am not sure in fact of the exact feelings but I – from more or less when she told me – I was happy because I wanted to enjoy a child since the age of 15. I longed for a child since that day! So, like um, I felt like shouting! I wanted the baby!

Lwethu: I was actually excited. I don't know why. I was in Grade 11. I was actually excited, because all my sisters have babies. So, I have love for children…You see, I wanted to experience how does it feel to – to take care of something that is my own blood, you see. Yah, my own flesh and blood…I was part excited, you see, but on the side I was thinking what does this do to my future, all of that. I thought of those things. But, it was okay in the long run.

Sadly, for most of these young men their initial excitement would turn to sadness. For Lwethu, his plans for 'having a successful life' ended when his child arrived while he was still at school (at age 18) and he made plans for getting a job to support his child. Despite passing matric, nearly a year later he remained unemployed and said that 'everything now is going down, down, down, down, down, down, down, down'. He laughed when he spoke of his career in 'loxion management' – a street-savvy euphemism for unemployment in the township – yet his demeanour changed as his words echoed those of many others, like Luthando:

Luthando: I'm a father. I can't do everything for my daughter. So, I just feel like a kid. I – I just feel small because – I can't look after my baby, you see?

For Lonwabo, who dropped out of school in Grade 9 and was training to become a traditional healer, having a child at 18, though unexpected, brought him initial happiness. His happiness soon turned to anguish as the mother of his child and her family rejected him in favour of another partner she had (at the same time):

Lonwabo: At that time [when the baby was born] I did have a relationship with her like, and the baby. I used to get to her place and change nappies or change the bathwater and stuff. Then eventually, her father started pushing me away, and – then I stopped going there…Her family doesn't think that I'm the father, neh! Cos the thing is, the other guy, neh, is a rich guy. He works for the government…[her] family is a high-class family of which I don't think they want anything to do with me!…her father also said that to me, that I am a drunkard!

Talk of termination of pregnancy

Despite these mainly strong (and negative) emotional responses to the initial news of their impending fatherhood, very few of these young fathers seriously entertained the idea of terminating the pregnancy – or even tried to convince their partners to terminate. Only three spoke of considering termination. Luthando went into some detail describing his and his partner's decision to terminate, which was thwarted by his mother:

Luthando: [When] we find out that she was three weeks pregnant…we came to a decision that we should [exhale breath] [pause]…we should – she should do the miscarriage thing. [pause] Abortion, yah. And then we agreed. So, we go back to the – the clinic. But then she was three months pregnant…So they send us to – [snaps fingers] what is this hospital? Groote Schuur, and we go there. And then they give us a date, that we going to come back there for abortion, yah. They give us a letter. But, I keep the letter in my pocket…Then I came back home. My mother [pause] knew that there was something bothering me, because I was – all the time I was just, heh, I was getting nervous – all the time…So, then she ask me then what's going on. And then I tell her that my girlfriend is pregnant…I decided to just tell her, tell her that we going to make an – that my girlfriend, she's going to do an abortion. So my mother told me that [pause]…you can't do an abortion [at three months]. 'Just let her give birth, and then the money that I have I'll just give to you and…you just going to raise the baby.' So then, we just gave it up. Then my mother told [me] that I should throw that letter away.

Sifiso: I had many thoughts running in my mind, I even thought of telling the girl to terminate the pregnancy. Yah, so I told her to do abortion but then she refused to do it. I spoke to my mom and she spoke to her [the girl's] parents and they all rejected the suggestion about terminating the pregnancy; they said the child will grow even though the situation isn't good. So I accepted that; so the girl didn't do abortion. So the child was born and she was alive. I was really stressed. I almost failed my matric.

Nhlanhla said that he 'told her to do an abortion…but I couldn't go through with it. So we just decided to keep the child', while Sakhile described how his partner 'was also thinking of terminating the pregnancy' but that his 'friends went to her and told her not to do such a thing'. Of the remaining young men, a further five spoke strongly against termination, reflecting his mother's view (Lwethu) and her mother's view (Onathi).

Lwethu: My mom was actually okay with it [the pregnancy]…because there's one thing she hates most, she hates abortions, you see? So she took it as a blessing that – I was gonna have the child, yah.

Onathi: We never thought of that [termination]. Actually, her mother told me that there's no way that she's doing that. Because, abortion is – can be very dangerous, can kill you, all that stuff. So, her mother didn't agree of that. So, no, we – we didn't talk about abortion at all. Her mother just said that it's not an option…Abortion is killing someone, so – I don't believe in it. No. What I believe in is that everything happens for a reason, so once I got her pregnant so be it. Don't kill a baby. Why should you kill a baby?

Only Tapelo, Yusuf and Zaid spoke of *their* unmediated conviction *against* having an abortion, despite what their partners may have wanted:

Tapelo: That's why I told myself, 'Okay, I can't say to her she must do an abortion, eh.' I told myself, 'Okay, I want my baby. That's my blood.' I told myself I don't want it [an abortion] even if she said she want it. I told her, 'No, this is my blood. *You can't just throw it away.*'

Yusuf: She also thought of abortion. Then I told her that there is no need for that and then the other day she asked me to buy her brandy to drink and maybe the baby will disappear. Then I told her that she was crazy.

Zaid: I won't even ask how far you are cos I won't have plans of killing the baby or anything like that. I don't have the heart to do that. Killing an innocent child that did nothing, didn't ask to be in this world or whatever. So I won't even ask.

Ibrahiem's mother was the only mother who asked 'do I want an abortion or do I want to keep the baby. Then I said I want to keep the baby and she said I must go find me a job, then we went to her [the girl's] mother and my mother came with. It was on a Sunday.' For the remaining 22 young fathers in this study, termination of pregnancy didn't come up in our conversation at all when they were asked to describe their experiences of young fatherhood – from the day they received the news to their current involvement in the life of their child. There was also no difference between 'black' and 'coloured' young men's attitudes towards termination.

The meaning of responsibility

Although the young men displayed strong emotions, most of which were negative, their discourse around taking responsibility for their child was strong. Only a handful spoke of thinking about denying paternity. Of course, this study's largest limitation is that those young men who have denied paternity are also unlikely to have volunteered to participate in a study of young fathers. Nevertheless, these young fathers' understanding of the meaning of responsibility provides a further example of the strong emotion which accompanied their talk of the experiences of being a young father in an impoverished community.

Why young fathers deny paternity

We asked why young fathers deny paternity. The answers circulated around two main issues: uncertainty about whether they were in fact the fathers and fear that they would be unable to financially support their children and so be shamed by the girl's family and their communities. Onathi explains both reasons:

Onathi: Guys run away because maybe they know the girlfriend is like seeing many people, so there's the doubting…so that's why the guys say, 'No man, that's not my baby'. That's why guys – some guys deny. Because they know that she isn't – she's not sleeping with him alone. She's sleeping with other guys. So why should she look at him as the father… Some guys run away when the baby's born [because] he like [thinks], 'No man, I don't have money, so I'm worse for my baby', so they run away. I think it's about pride…Like they say, 'No man, I will lose my respect if I can't support. What will people say about me on the streets?' All that stuff.

Two young men spoke of their confusion because they were now with other partners, which contributed to them initially denying paternity before relenting and taking responsibility. Nhlanhla explains:

Nhlanhla: At first I also wanted to deny because I had a girlfriend [pause] that I thought she was much better than her [the one I got pregnant]. She was beautiful, she is good-looking, had good stuff – great family, good background. So when my girlfriend was pregnant [pause] I didn't want to tell Nee that I have made Gee pregnant, because they knew each other. So what I did was [pause] I told her that it was not mine. So she told me that it was mine [pause]. So then I told her [pause] it's fine [pause] I'll see when the child is born.

Waiting until the baby was born seemed to be a common occurrence, especially among young men who were unsure about whether they were in fact the father of the child, or with young men who were afraid of their ability to support the child:

Bongani: Ehh, I partially denied it [pause] but after the baby was born I saw it, and my parents also said the child looks like me. Maybe it was because of the things she was doing [having other partners] that made me deny the child at first.

Dumisani: She shouted me too much, too much…I'm not saying that I'm denying the child but at the moment, it's better if we wait until the child is born. That is what I said to her mom…I was afraid to tell that to them [that the child is mine] because they will expect too much from me whereas I didn't have much to support.

Why young men embrace their children

Young men spoke of three main reasons for why they *accepted* a child as theirs: knowledge that they had made the girl pregnant; the role of their fathers in their lives (and their desire to rescue and transform this experience); and fear of the consequences of denying the child. Most told of how they knew without a doubt that the child was theirs, because they knew that they had been sleeping with the mother without a condom or that the condom had failed.

Jabu: The reason why I – it seemed like I had no choice but to admit. I knew it was my fault. So there was no way I could say no.

Luthando: I can't deny something, *neh*. I must admit what I did and I know she's my girlfriend. She was with me. And I won't like to do that to her.

Nhlanhla: I felt like running away [laughs]. I thought of denying everything, actually I did deny at first…But then when it was close to the due date, I knew it was my child.

Andile: I told myself that the baby is mine and I am going to take responsibility…because the child was made by me and I told myself that whatever happens I'll be there.

Many spoke of the fact that their fathers had been a key reason for them accepting paternity and responsibility. Ironically, some young fathers explained that it was the fact that their father had not denied paternity that encouraged them to accept paternity and the role of a father, while others argued the exact opposite. It was the fact that their fathers were absent from their lives that led them to want things to be different for their own children.

Onathi, Siya and Jabu explained further:

Onathi: The reason why I didn't run away, because I knew that – I just got the feeling that the baby, yah, it is mine. So like, my father didn't do it to me, so why should I do it to her? My father didn't run away. He stood up and faced the consequences of a baby, so why should I run away from her? So I didn't run.

Siya: [Why I never denied] I think it's the problem of my father. The problem I told you, eh, earlier about my father [disappearing]. So I like – the pain I felt, um, I came to acknowledge that no one should feel the pain that I felt because it was very painful. So that's when I, um, I decided no man, I need to accept this. Because really, for my child to go through with the way that, um, the pain that I went through; it's not fair.

Jabu: Because you see when – when you – you grow up with your mother, and your mother tell you the things, you know, that you one day when you – you have the family, you must be present for your baby. And support, uh, you know, and be a responsible man.

Dumisani alluded to cultural traditions ('I think rejecting a child [pause] in amaZulu culture could cause you problems – you find that things are not going alright'). Others spoke of the 'bad luck' rejecting a child would bring. Xolile expanded on this by telling a story of the consequences of denial:

Xolile: I had friend that stay in Site B, in T-Section. He denied – he denied he made the girlfriend pregnant. And he got twins. After that, his girlfriend's mother told him that 'I will see that you not gonna last in life'. It was just after two weeks, and then [claps his hands once] and then we – hear he was dead…He was drinking, then go outside to pee. When he look out at the back, another guy just took a knife and stabbed him – dead.

The discourse of 'responsibility'

No matter what the reason for young men accepting their children, the strongest discourse remained one of 'responsibility'. Each young man, when asked about his response to the news of his impending fatherhood, spoke in some terms of a sense of responsibility for the coming child:

Lwethu: It's a matter of responsibility…I knew what I was doing.

Tapelo: I know I've been sleeping with that girl and I didn't wear a condom so she came to me and told me that she is pregnant…Everything your child needs you must be there for him. You must do everything for the child.

When asked where this sense of responsibility came from, young men frequently referred to the advice received from their parents. Sifiso and Ibrahiem explained at length:

Sifiso: I would say in the family that brought me up [pause] as you grow up you are told how to behave yourself as young man; and if you get a child, if it's yours, you shouldn't reject it [pause] you have to take responsibility. So [pause] I also grew up with that mindset that if I bring someone on earth [pause] I have to accept that I'm a father now. I must raise my child. So, I can say that it's that [pause] that made me not to deny my child [and be responsible].

Ibrahiem: [My mother said] it's not easy to be a father, and it's not just for now – tomorrow it's not done. It will be like this for the rest of your life. And I must take responsibility…I felt like I have a responsibility and I must stop with all my stuff because I have a baby and I must go work.

For the majority of young men this sense of responsibility was tied in to their sense of masculinity. Frequently, the words 'responsible' (or 'responsibility') and 'man' were used in the same sentence:

Marlin: Like a responsible man…Act like a grown man. Show her the right way.

Jabu: You must be present for your baby, and support, you know, and be a responsible man.

Sifiso: The advice he [stepfather] gave me is that I'm a grown-up now – I'm a man – I have to be responsible.

Parents parenting children's children

However, especially among the 'black' young fathers who were still in school, responsibility was easily ceded to their parents, often at their parents' initiation:

Xolile: After that, my father told me no. He's going to take the responsibility – the responsibility for me, for what I did…And my mother, and they still support my child right now.

Saki: It was my mother's responsibility to do everything for my son…She made me believe that she'd take care of my son. I must focus on my studies. I must make something of myself. If I keep on telling myself that I have a responsibility, that would have been a problem for me. I was very young then. I think what I've done is the best thing.

Young fathers explained that their parents' investment in their children was in order for them to have a better life than their parents had had. By looking after their son's child now, parents were enabling their son to complete school and become more than 'grass cutters' or 'shepherds'.

Reasons for having a child at a young age

Towards the end of the study, young fathers were asked why they thought young people become parents. Each respondent answered the question quickly and confidently, and Sifiso captured almost all of the reasons in his response:

Sifiso: The cause of young people to become parents at a young age [pause] it is to be exposed to many things when you are still young and also [pause] being careless when doing certain things – like not using condoms and not listening to your parents when they advise you. And sometimes [pause] someone might see his/her friend having a child [pause] and also decides to have a child too. So it could be peer pressure; I think that is what causes young people to be parents. And sometimes they see themselves as adults [pause] – sometimes it's a mistake. It's things like that…Like to be exposed to things like alcohol and drugs and going to clubs and all that. So after a person has had a couple of drinks and there are girls here, he becomes horny and they end up having sex without protection. And the girl falls pregnant, then they become parents at a young age.

For most, alcohol and not using condoms were the chief reasons. But a number also spoke of young people *wanting* children (both young men and young women); of pregnancy as being 'a fashion'; of pregnancy being 'the girls' fault' (the way they dress, loving money, and wanting a child grant); of young people's ignorance about biology and contraception; and of young people's sense of invulnerability – 'it won't happen to me, I'm still young'.

Alcohol

For Jabu, Sifiso and Nhlanhla, going to a party, a nightclub and a matric dance respectively, getting drunk and having unprotected sex with a girl with whom they were not in a relationship, resulted in their child or, in the words of Nhlanhla, 'So boom the baby came!' Vuyo admitted that mixing alcohol and sex is 'careless' because 'you forget about a condom'. Lonwabo spoke in greater detail about why alcohol is so prevalent among young men in his community:

Lonwabo: The thing is – financial – that's what I'm saying. Like, I can't do anything about [it] myself!…I [have] too many problems of which sometimes I get over them by drinking!

He continued to say that alcohol, and frequently *dagga* (cannabis) and *tik* (crystal meth), 'pushes you to do something you already wanted to do. It gives you the courage…to talk to a girl until she says yes [to sex]'. His own sexual relationship with 'the mother of my child is like…based on like when maybe we were drunk then we did this thing – sleep together, but when we were like maybe sober, we don't go at each other'. Finally, Lwethu alluded to the fact that the difference between young men in the suburbs and young men in the townships is that of material wealth:

Lwethu: Let's take a guy from the suburbs and take a guy from here [township]. There he gets everything – everything he wants he has – there's no problems, no worries, no anything. But at this side, you don't get everything you want, you see? So you go drown your sorrows in alcohol, you see, just to carry the stress, be okay. You end up being an alcoholic and all that. You do things, you see?

No condoms

Young men spoke about why there seemed to be such a reluctance to use condoms among them as a group. For young 'black' men, the idea of pleasure dominated – having sex 'skin to skin', 'meat to meat' or 'm-to-m' resulted in increased pleasure during the sex act. A number of other young men also spoke of the pleasure of having sex without a condom:

Vuyo: Because it's, eh, it's very good when – when it's very – feel – you feel it without a condom – more than [when] you use a condom. I knew about condom. I had condom in my pocket. But I didn't use it.

Onathi: Condom is like having a sweet with a wrapper on, so I don't use a condom…Not use a condom is nice. You can feel that you're doing something. So you want to experience that and see how it feels.

Xolile related how when a partner asked him to use a condom, he put one on at the beginning and then before entering her took it off again without her seeing. Lwandile pled ignorance of condoms at first:

Lwandile: When we started to have, uh, sex and all of those stuff. Then, uh, I wasn't really aware about this thing condom. So, I was doing meat-to-meat, without it. We call it 'm-to-m' or 's-to-s' – skin-to-skin', yah…I was 15. So in 2006, that's when our relationship started to be like a thick thing. There was no condom. Because I was coming from rural areas, I was not aware of those – and I was young.

But S'bu concluded that young men have 'enough knowledge' of condoms and even carry condoms around with them, but that frequently girlfriends don't want to use them; they remain in the pocket of their jeans or, in the heat of the moment, they can't be found, as in Siya's case:

Siya: It was raining and cold, so, um, we went over to my place. So I normally have a box of condoms but I don't know what happened to them that day, I couldn't find them. It was just a one-off thing and then we agreed that we were not going to use a condom. Um, and then that's how it happened.

Bongani: I had enough knowledge about that; but the problem is that the condom burst the first time. And when we did it the second round, she did not want me to use a condom.

Zaid explained that frequently when the opportunity for sex arrives, there are no condoms around and so young people are willing to risk it for the sake of consummating desire:

Zaid: It comes [the opportunity] just as you don't have condoms on you or she don't have condoms on her. Now this is the only chance you get because there's *mos* now no one at home or whatever and then they maybe talk. If anything happens now, and then they stand for it or whatever. And then maybe she say yes, and you just go for it and then it maybe just happen. The – she just falls pregnant by that one chance, that one time you didn't use a condom.

Xolile related his father's harsh words when he eventually told them he had impregnated a girl and that it was a mistake. His father's reply was that 'this [was] not a mistake, because you know that there is a condoms. Why didn't [you] use a condom?' His reply was 'I don't know', but in fact the truth was more culpable. Xolile explained that not using condoms is a way in which to impress your friends: 'Other guys they say I'm just wasting my sperm [by using a condom]. So, you try to impress [them]. You don't think about…these STD [sexually transmitted disease] or HIV and AIDS.'

Other young men also explained that not using a condom was a matter of trust:

Luxolo: No, she was a permanent girlfriend…[so] I was usually having sex without condom. Because I loved her and I trusted her. You see?

The problem arose when young men began to use condoms as a barometer of trust and felt forced into not using condoms with second or third concurrent partners, out of fear their partners would accuse them of being unfaithful because of using a condom. Only two young fathers reported condom failure ('condom burst') as the reason for their impregnation. The remainder had all not used condoms, and only two had not done so in the hopes of having a child.

Ignorance and a sense of invulnerability

The theme of ignorance was picked up by numerous young men, who frequently admitted their own stupidity and ignorance:

Ntombisa: I played that something you can call *undize* [hide and seek] and *eish* [pause]…we were kids. I did not know that there was going to be a child in what we were doing…It was just *undize*. We were kids. It still eats me inside what I have done because…that girl's family calls me notorious.

Tapelo: I didn't know at the time, at that time I could have a baby.

Luxolo: I didn't believe I can make somebody pregnant, because I'm still young – I was stupid.

Lwandile: It comes to a lack of knowledge – it's whereby you don't know what will be the conse-quences of what you have done.

Such ignorance is difficult to understand in an age of prolific sex education, especially when the young men concerned are 15, 16 and 17 years old (Lwandile 15, Tapelo 17, Luxolo 17, Ntombisa 16). Two possible explanations for such ignorance are possible. Firstly, young fathers who spent most of their schooling in rural areas were more likely to speak of their own ignorance. Secondly, many of these young men were in lower grades than their ages suggested, and it is possible that the sex education they received was inadequate to their physical maturity. Although some were ignorant of the biology of producing children, others – like Lungile and Onathi – believed themselves to be invulnerable to the consequences of having sex without using condoms or other contraception:

Lungile: I had knowledge about such things but I didn't think it would happen. Because I was still young; I didn't know it would happen.

Onathi: I was drinking, I didn't use condoms – I told myself, 'Nah man, it won't happen. Why happen to me? Like, it's not my first time not using condom, so it won't happen to me.'

Wanting a child

Rather surprisingly, a number of young men spoke about young people wanting babies for a variety of reasons. Chief among these was to keep a partner. Luthando recounted how his girlfriend told him 'she thinks that we should become parents' before he went to the bush because 'she loves me too much. So she was afraid that I should find another girlfriend.' Onathi elaborated on this theme by confirming the view that girls 'want to get pregnant…to trap him' but also argued that:

Onathi: I don't think for guys it's always a mistake. Some guys want to have babies. 'I want to know how to be a father', all that stuff. 'All my friends have babies, why shouldn't I?'

Onathi then concluded by telling me that he had 'five friends' with babies and that 'there's only one friend who doesn't have a baby'. This proved to be true throughout the study, with many of the young men who were participating recruiting other participants from among their close friends.

Sabier frankly admitted that he wanted a baby to keep his girlfriend:

Sabier: A lot of boys wanted her and she wanted me. So I thought no I'm not going to [lose her] – I liked her…I just told her that can we make the baby, so she said yes.

A number of the young 'coloured' men, like Marlin, said they wanted to have children because they might not live long enough to wait for a child due to the dangers of gang violence in their areas:

Marlin: They want to [pause] experience it before the time…[You don't know] if you will live or not. You could be younger than 20 and something could happen to you. Then you didn't leave anything behind. People's situations – everyone in townships become gangsters if they leave school. This is how a lot of them die. And before they die, they want to have a little one of their own…Cos in our neighbourhood there's dangerous gun shooting and there are many gangsters. Young guys, 15, 16, that have big guns and shoot at the police [pause]. They get shot dead [pause] because they don't have a life.

Xolile: I want when I'm dead there's another Xolile there on earth. You see?…So see, we don't like to use a condom…maybe this is my last chance to make a baby.

Lwethu, Xolile and Tapelo spoke of pregnancy as 'a fashion' (see Swartz 2009), 'like if you don't have a baby now, then you are behind so you must have a baby, so then you are in fashion' (Onathi). For Sakhile, having a child even though he was in school was because 'I found someone that I really liked. We went to the same school and she was well behaved and I wished that I could have a child with her; it's not that it was a mistake. And my wishes came true. Because another thing I wished for was, it will happen that I will have a child [while] my parents are alive.' Andile also admitted that 'I decided that I was going to be a father of a child – I meant it – I wanted to experience life'. Lwethu summed up by saying: 'You can't say no if a girl says, "I want your baby," you see? They do that nowadays.'

The environment and a lack of guidance from parents and teachers

Young men also blamed the environment in which they lived, claiming that young people were exposed to sex at a much younger age through what they saw happening in their communities and on television. Jabu said that children 'in our communities…are *ou papa* – forward – they [like] to do things before time', while Sakhile spoke of how parents and teachers failed children:

Sakhile: For them to have children early? [pause] I would say it's the ways things are now, things have changed [pause]. Like even that they start dating at a young age [pause] and also that parents aren't strict enough. A child comes home late and the mother doesn't ask where she comes from…I also think there isn't respect any more…Even in schools. In the past at school you used to feel like you are at home – your teacher becomes like your parent. Others would even visit your home to talk to your parents. Now they don't care…Because you find that the teacher knows that a certain child is having an affair at school but he doesn't tell the child's parents.

Numerous young men referred to the absence of any discussion about sex and its consequences when they were growing up. Young 'black' men referred to it as being 'against our tradition' for adults and children to talk about sex, but 'coloured' young men also spoke of how any discussion about sex and contraception was similarly absent or rare in their families.

Xolile: The reason that we're having sex too much, it's our parents didn't even want to sit us at the table to talk about sex…our parents – they have that minds of the old age. They didn't even talk about that – that you can get AIDS.

Siya: Mostly the things make them to become young parents that they lack guidance from their parents. So that leads them to be young parents. If, if a father can be there or a mother can be there for a child…I don't think one can go and be a young father if they can be there and show them the consequences of being a young father and a mother!…If my father was there telling me…I don't think I would be a father today! But he was not there. Then I became a father because I had no one to tell me this is wrong and this was right because my brothers were just influencing me and doing what they do the best – and it's girls.

At the same time, Lwethu captured the struggle going on in pride-filled young people when he said:

Lwethu: In terms of…young people, if you tell them to do something, they're going to do the oppo-site, you see?…It's because we don't like to be told what to do. You want to do your own thing, you see? So, if you tell me – I'm gonna show you – even though it's gonna affect me during the long run. You tell that stuff, I'm gonna show you I'm not, cos you have that pride. You don't want to be told what to say – and what to do.

It's the girls' fault

For Xolile, it was because 'these young girls, they love a lot of money' and so frequent taverns where they think they can pick up wealthy guys who will buy them drinks and spend money on them in return for sex. He furthered his argument by telling of a teacher at school who 'was having a relationship with a 13-year-old girl':

Xolile: And when the community people found out this girl was pregnant, so they ask her who make you pregnant, she said no, it's my teacher. But all along, her mother knows about their relationship. And after the community ask her why she allow it, and she said, 'Just mind your business, not mine…because now we are in negotiations about *ilobolo*.' How can she negotiate about *ilobolo* for a 13-year-old girl?…Because this new guy now, he have the money, everything. And he buy the groceries.

Xolile also argued that:

Xolile: Some of the girls, not all of the girls…come with short, short skirt at school. She show us all the butt now. You see? So now, if I can't concentrate…because when they just dress like that, then they show us they just want to have sex with us. You just want to show us to follow behind after you now.

Six of the 27 young fathers spoke of how young women get pregnant because of the prospect of getting a child grant (despite evidence to the contrary).[15] Dumisani's, Tapelo's and Marlin's views were echoed by Xolile, Sakhile and Vuyo, who recommended that 'Parliament' should stop grants for young parents:

Dumisani: You see a young person who is around 18 years old [pause] and she has two children. Sure that person didn't have a child by mistake [pause] but she was probably looking at the grant.

Tapelo: See some of them, there is that money coming from the government so some of them want that money. That's why they get [pregnant] because some of them they don't go to school, they just sit around. They do it for that because some of the children here don't go to school, they just drink.

Marlin: Everywhere. In all the townships. Manenberg, Mitchell's Plain, Bishop Lavis, everywhere. They stand in a line, 16-, 17-year-olds and pregnant. It's R300 a child…Now most of the girls misuse the money. Misuse their bodies to have children – to get money – money for luxuries.

The impact of the event on young men's lives

During final interviews, the 27 young fathers were asked to reflect on the ways in which the arrival of their child had changed their lives. All but three had much to say, mainly surrounding their use of money and alcohol, social activities as well as some more emotional issues such as damage to their reputation and how it forced them to be 'grown up'.

Of the three young men who told us that their lives had not changed, Lonwabo asserted that 'it hasn't, because I didn't – play any part of being the father. Maybe it would've changed my life if I did play the role – that role. But for now, nothing.' (Lonwabo was the young man who had been pushed aside by the family of the mother of his child, who refused him access and ultimately denied that he was the father of the child.) For the other two young men – Sakhile and Saki – both had their child looked after by their parents. Both sets of parents were together and living in a rural area.

Saki: Not really. Nothing…nothing. My life just continued with the same. It's a good thing. It's a good thing to continue life, because life doesn't end for me, when I got my child. So it had to continue. So, just like that. I've got the support from my parents.

Sakhile: What can I say? [pause] It didn't change my life that much because [pause] I didn't have time to be closer to her [my child]. I've always been away from her since she was a baby.

15 A series of studies (DoSD 2006; Makiwane & Udjo 2006; Moultrie & McGrath 2007) have shown that the child support grant is not a 'perverse incentive' for increased teen fertility. In fact, teenage fertility has been on the decline since the inception of the grant.

Now my life is still the way it was before. There is nothing – besides the things I've been getting – that's where I can say things have changed. At home they don't buy me things any more. Instead of providing for me, they provide for my child and I have to see for myself.

Changed financial and employment priorities

By far the largest group of young fathers referred to the increasing importance that money now played in their lives, since they no longer needed to use it just on themselves but also on their child:

Luxolo: The difference, you know, once I have a child…everything you do once you have the money – the first is the child.

Lwandile: I could say in a financial way! Cos I – if I want something I've – they will tell me that ok if you want this, er, what will your child get? So, we need what we had to give you so that you can give more to the child. Because you are not working now and the child needs some supports.

Tapelo: I know I've got a responsibility. I know I got a child. Even when I have money I know that this money is for the child.

Secondly, although almost all had supportive parents, these parents had redirected the support they had previously given to their son, to their son's child. Young men spoke sadly about how they were now seldom able to buy any new clothes for themselves because of the baby:

Zaid: [When] my mommy take us out for shopping then I *mos* know now I'm gonna get now a pair of *takkies* [running shoes]. No. Nothing like that. I don't even ask any more for stuff. It's just – I'll just tell her what the baby need, man.

Dumisani: Like having money [pause] if I have money I would buy things for myself only [pause]. Like buying clothes for myself and buy things that would make me happy. But now I have to think about my child, who is supposed to get nice things and [pause] I will do mine stuff later.

Luthando: I felt like, yah, sometimes I felt that…this is going to change my life. See, because [pause] I can't get all the things that I was – all the things that I was asking from my mother now. My mother used to give me money to buy myself clothes. But now she can't. [Because] there is the kid and the kid needs the money for food and the clothes [mumbles].Yeah, I'm suffering a lot.

Vuyo: I suffering because I've got a baby. [My father] say, 'I can't buy you a Nike *takkie*, because now you got a baby. I buy for your baby, not for you.'

Sakhile: I do things for myself because whenever I ask for something at home they say they will only do things for my child, not me.

Related to the changes both in the ways in which they viewed money and in how their own financial circumstances changed was the change in their attitude towards the future and future employment:

Jabu: I'm now responsible. I know I have to work. Whatever I do is not for me only. I also think for him.

Lwethu: It's different in a way that I used to do…Like, let's say, for instance, looking for a job, or anything. I didn't care because I know my mom will provide for me, you see? But now that she's here [my child] – I know she's not going to be here just for a year. She's gonna be here forever and ever and ever. So, I have to stand up for myself and look for a job next year. Next year I have been planning to go back to school. But it's hard. It's hard. It's hard. To find a job. To fund school. Because everything needs money, money, money, money, money…and it's hard. It's hard, very hard.

Three young men also spoke of how the child's arrival had put paid to their plans for furthering their studies or completing school, while Bongani described how he had to devise a plan to study part-time instead of full-time in order to work to support the child:

Lungile: It has changed my life a lot [pause] because [pause] I still wanted to study and finish school [pause]. So I had to drop out of school because of him.

Nhlanhla: I've lost out on many things like my future plans and stuff, but I wouldn't say I'm regretting, because I can manage. It's not that bad for me.

Bongani: I was thinking of studying, but because I have to support the child and pay things like that, I have to study part-time. I was thinking of doing the jobs that are easy to do, like being a policeman or a firefighter; do jobs like that while I continue with my studies [but I really want to be] a civil engineer.

Changes in social activities

For all three groups of young men – in Langa, Bonteheuwel and Cato Manor/Mayville – having a child curtailed their social activities in at least three ways. Firstly, their weekends changed since they now included seeing their child and, if they were together with the mother of their child, visiting her as well.

Andile: When I didn't have a child I like to walk around a lot. Now that I have a child I stay at home most of the time. My weekends were busy and I use to come home in the mornings, but I don't do that any more.

Dumisani: But most of the time before I had a child I was at home or at school, and weekends I spent most playing soccer at the playgrounds. Most weekends I was at the playgrounds and I enjoyed being there [pause]. I didn't have any problems. But now though I do attend other things, but most of the time I use weekends to make money, because I get casual jobs over the weekend most of the time, you see.

Nhlanhla: I'll say a weekend now is different from a weekend before, because a weekend before I would wake up on Monday without a cent. No money in the bank and I also don't have money, you see? And now I know that when I wake on Monday, I know I have at least R100 in my pocket. Even when my child wants some chips [pause] I'll be able to buy him.

Fadiel: I can't go out like I used to any more with my friends. A typical weekend before my children were born I would go out with my friends every day of the weekend and buy myself things all the time. I only had to see to myself. Now, all my money goes to my children and to care for them. I can't go out like I want any more because I have responsibilities now. All I think about is how I can provide for my children.

Yusuf: Then I was just on the go. Now I'm on go slow. Yes. But because – it's as if I'm gonna take the money that I have and party it out, but I don't know how my child is doing. What does she need, um, clothes, panties, things like that.

Secondly, since they had less money they tended to go out less and consume less alcohol – the latter also due to the fact that they now needed to think not only of themselves but also of the child:

Vuyo: When I get maybe R20, I think about See [my child]. Then, maybe she don't have, eh, Pampers [nappies]. Can't buy alcohol. So, I can't go to Licks's [tavern]. So – cos, I don't have a money. No, now I go to buy a Pampers [nappies].

S'bu: Because the things I use to do before I don't do them any more. Like going out at night to drink alcohol. When we get paid [pause] – when my friends get paid [pause] we go and have drinks. Friday, Saturday I'm drunk. I don't do that any more.

Sifiso and Onathi spoke of not wanting to be involved in dangerous activities such as drinking in taverns or stealing, since they don't want their children to grow up without a father:

Sifiso: It did change it in a way [pause] because now I know there is a person I've brought on earth, so I must try and avoid other things like – I'm trying to behave and take care of myself. Not do things that will put me into trouble. Like be naughty and all that, and maybe doing things that will put my life into danger and end up dying and my child grow up without a father. Like going out for drinks at night with friends; maybe go steal [pause] things like that. I left all those things and I told myself that I want to live an innocent life.

Onathi: I'm not drinking a lot now [that my son is born]. Because I'm scared, like, maybe I get shot, something bad happen to me. So like, my boy will grow up without a father. So that's why I don't drink too much now. But I do drink, but not much. I'm afraid something bad happen. But bad things happen inside there, in the *shebeens* [taverns] there. Especially Licks – Licks is dangerous. But we have fun there. But it is dangerous. So, I don't want my boy to grow up without a father.

Sadly, Onathi's own father, with whom he lived, was shot and killed in a hijacking in Gugulethu while Onathi was completing his social network interviews.

Growing up, reasoning and restoring reputations

A few young men recorded other changes in their lives, including Siya, who spoke of how having a child at the age of 14 damaged his reputation among the community organisations with whom he worked in the Eastern Cape:

Siya: Um, negatively it affected my life because, like I was known as the guy who preaches that people should lead a life whereby they won't let themselves down later…It was very hard for the community to understand that I made [such a mistake]. I was like the most demotivated, I didn't like [to] talk to many people. Many organisations were no longer negotiating with me because of what I did…So that the effect that it had on my life was to destroy my reputation.

Along with Lungile and S'bu, he continued to speak of how having a child had changed his life by forcing him to 'make me reason very much', to 'act like a grown-up' (S'bu), and to be 'in charge of my life' and not 'rely on parents for help or advice' (Lungile).

Conclusion

This chapter began by describing the strong emotion that characterised young men's narratives of becoming and being fathers, and which was evident throughout as they described their fear of their parents and the shame that they brought to families with strong traditional and cultural values. While this was most evident among 'black' young men, many 'coloured' young fathers spoke of the strong Muslim and Christian religious values they feared transgressing. This is a surprising finding, since stereotypically it is the young women who fear shame and rejection. So, while researchers such as Fry and Trifiletti (1983) document young fathers' stress, anxiety and fear of rejection due to being unable to provide for their child, the literature is quiet on the sense of shame young men from traditional or religious cultures display at the news of a mistimed child. A possible explanation[16] for these young fathers' response, especially 'black' young men, could lie in the strong bonds of mutual trust and respect that exist in collectivist and traditional cultures. Pregnancy has financial and moral implications for a young man's family that extend beyond the present. Cultural practices of not introducing the child to the ancestors and not being able to name a child until cultural rites have been fulfilled, all bring displeasure to families soaked in these traditions – and shame and fear to their sons.

Of course, not all responses are negative. Young men's discourse of responsibility was strong and passionate, though seldom recorded in the literature. Also, some young men claim that they wanted to have a child while young – a characteristic confirmed in a study among young urban African American fathers (Davies et al. 2004) – largely due to the uncertainty of their life circumstances. The literature also confirms these young fathers' contentions that the two primary reasons why young men become fathers at an early age are the ubiquitous presence of alcohol in their lives, which inevitably leads to greater sexual risk taking, and a lack of condom or other contraceptive use (Nagy & Dunn 1999; Santelli et al. 2001; Stueve & O'Donnell 2005). Also positive is young men's assertion that having a child motivates many to change their life choices, especially regarding substance use, violence and risky sexual activity (Lesser et al. 2001). While these young men confirm this finding, some also speak of the ways in which hearing the news overwhelmed them, resulting in depression and thoughts of suicide. This latter issue, that of the mental health of young fathers, is seldom addressed, largely because young men talk of their needs in practical rather than psychosocial terms (see the next chapter). This was confirmed in a study by Weinman et al. (2005), which found that although young fathers identified feeling angry, sad, depressed, helpless and stressed, few asked for help for these mental health issues. Instead, their most frequently requested service needs were related to jobs and skills training – a topic which Chapter 4 addresses in some depth.

16 During the debriefing and consultation workshop this issue was repeatedly raised by researchers in an attempt to get young fathers to offer a plausible explanation for their inordinate fear and sense of shame, but none was forthcoming except for the financial hardship they would bring on their families.

CHAPTER 4

'Being there and providing; that's my job': Young fathers' perspectives on good fathering

The previous chapter discussed the mass of emotion involved in young impoverished 'black' and 'coloured' fathers' experiences of becoming fathers in the South African context. This challenges the media portrayals of the irresponsible young 'black' male who impregnates a young woman and then simply disappears, leaving countless children fatherless in communities that badly need male role models. In this chapter, the focus shifts from the multiple emotions that young fathers experience in coming to terms with being the father of a child, and explores their understanding of what it *means* to be a good father, what it *takes* to be a good father and the extent to which their own fathering experiences affect their current understandings and practices.

Becoming a father in the context of absent fathers

The young fathers in this study provided an enormous amount of data about their own fathers, despite the fact that there were no direct questions in either of the individual interviews about their relationships with their own fathers. However, it seems that in the context of reflecting on their own experience of fatherhood, young men told important stories about their relationships with their own fathers. Table 4.1 provides a brief summary of the 27 young men in the study's experience of being fathered.

Just over one-third of the young men in the study grew up with a father mostly present in their household, while nearly two-thirds did not. There are arguably four kinds of absence that this latter group experienced: absence through death, absence with occasional contact, absence with regular contact, and absence with no contact at all. In this study, four young men had lost their fathers to death; a further four had occasional contact with their fathers (at least once a year); three had regular contact with their fathers; and six had no contact at all or never knew their fathers.

TABLE 4.1   *Respondents' experiences of being fathered*

Relationship with own father	Number of young men	%
Absent – deceased	4	15
Absent – never known or no contact	6	22
Absent – occasional contact	4	15
Absent – regular contact	3	11
Present	10	37

At least one young father, who had had no previous contact with his father, had recently resumed contact at the age of 15. So it came as no surprise that young men divided their fathering experiences into less stark categories than 'absent' or 'present' as they recounted their shifting relationships with their fathers, which changed as fathers returned home, left home, made contact after years of silence, died or moved in with 'girlfriends'. In addition, they had a number of labels for 'present' fathers. Heuristically, these categories can be described as 'financial fathers', 'angry fathers', 'faithless fathers' and 'talking fathers'.[17] The clearest category remained that of the 'absent father' – the father whom the young men in the study either never knew at all, or only recently came to know. Lwandile, Siya and Lonwabo describe the effect that this circumstance had on their lives and on their perspectives on fatherhood.

Lwandile, 17 years old at the time of the study and in Grade 11, lost his mother when he was seven years old and never knew his father. He became a father at the age of 15 after a long friendship with a girl in his neighbourhood. He says he was ignorant about sex and contraception at the time. He told his story eloquently, highlighting how growing up with an absent father meant that he had to 'steal time' from his uncles and grandfather, and that this had motivated him to be a 'present father' in the future to his own child:

Lwandile: My father – absent. I don't know where his is. And [pause] I didn't even see him when I was young until now. I saw those people who try [to] find [their] father. And, uh, I thought to myself no, he didn't even see me when I was young. Maybe he died or something. But I can't, uh, approach someone, uh, I don't know. Maybe he can say, 'No, you must go away. I don't know you.'…[But] I don't think there is a problem. Because my grandfather is there. So he does everything. If I need anything, he does everything for me…It's obvious I will be a present father in the future [laughs]. Because I saw that…having an absent father, it's like…my uncles, they don't have enough time to, like, speak with me. But *I used to steal their time* because they have their children. I could see that, even though they don't say that.

Siya's story is similar, although he became a father at the age of 14, after having multiple partners. He spoke of having a different partner for every day of the week and that 'I used to call them, like, by the days of the week. So I was only just left with Monday and Friday without someone.' He continued his story:

Siya: In Aliwal North I was…raised by my mom so I didn't see my father. So [when he came back] I was like, 'Where were you when I was like growing up?' For me to have a father figure in my life I had to use my older brothers and my grandfather.

Siya attributed his rampant sexual activity (he described himself as a *pleya*) at such a young age to the example of his older brothers, and the lack of guidance from a father. However, after he became a father, he became involved in an (almost) exclusive relationship with the mother of his child and was materially and emotionally involved in the life of his son, despite still being at school. He provided an analysis of what motivated him to change:

Siya: Despite the fact that I'm still a kid myself, it's great because I tend to know things and I tend to, like, know about what my father didn't give to me. Now I'm doing well being a father to my child, not like my own father did…To tell you the truth, the person who helped me

---

17   During the debriefing and consultation workshop, young men said that while 'talking fathers' captured the positive experience of fathers, they would also add 'caring fathers' and 'friendly fathers' to the list of positive types of fathers, while 'drinking fathers' must be added to their experience of failed fathering.

be the good father is my father! Because of the things he did to me before I became a man that made me be a very good father. Because if he was there for me, I don't think I would be there for Lee [my son] today! He wasn't there for me – so I felt that gap…So I don't want my child to feel the very same pain, because believe me it's very painful.

Lonwabo, who became a father at the age of 18 only to have his paternity rejected by his MOC's family, tells a more heart-wrenching story. He, too, grew up with an absent father:

Lonwabo: I grew up without a father in my life. So I don't want to do that for him [my son]…To be a good father [myself] – the things that I did not get from him – I wish I could give back, like, to my son…But ultimately I can't [pause] because I've been pushed away.

Lonwabo, now married to another woman, eloquently describes the pain of growing up with an absent father:

Lonwabo: From my experience, *neh*, from like my father not being there for me, like [pause] some-times like I ask myself, 'Is it me?' or 'What did I do?'…Because the symptoms are there… like lack of love from him and, uh, I don't know. Like for me now, *neh*…I don't want to talk to my mother. I just want to, like, to talk to my father. Like, there are many things that even now I want to talk to my father about…I wish I could have bonded with my father growing [up]. I missed all that. I missed all that…I am longing for that father bond! So, I wanted to give like that to my babies, any babies actually.

'Financial fathers', the second category young fathers described, are those who provided financially but were otherwise emotionally uninvolved in the lives of their children. This kind of father was also described as a 'quiet father', not talking to his children or taking an interest in their lives. Young men with these kinds of fathers spoke appreciatively about these men but without much emotion, a point which will be further discussed in the young men's own conception of what it means to be a good father, i.e. to provide financially:

Saki: No, he – the only thing he said [was] that he's willing to support me, as long as I don't drop out.

Sifiso: We see each other often and he assists me financially.

The third category of father that young men referred to could be termed the 'faithless father' – the father who had multiple 'girlfriends', who cheated on their current spouse, and who had many children, frequently with different women. Young men spoke of these kinds of fathers in critical terms, even if they themselves were engaged in MCPs.

Lwethu became a father at the age of 18 after one of his partners miscarried when he was 17. At the time of the study, he had four concurrent partners and was not in a steady relationship with any of them. He said he took it 'very hard' when someone broke up with him, and so decided to maintain a number of casual relationships that caused no emotional heartache. Luthando was in an exclusive partnership but spoke rather angrily about how his father had left his mother when he was five years old, and how he had found out that his father had had another partner at the same time as his mother, because he has a brother only one week older than him. Xolile, in turn, vacillated between anger and sadness at his father's extramarital affair, which resulted in a child and his parents' rocky marriage. Finally, both Xolile and Sabier became fathers at 17, and both had steady relationships with the mother of their child (although Xolile's was not exclusive).

Lwethu: [My father is] not married. [He has] four girlfriends. He has his own house. It's quite complicated because my dad has…12, 13 children…he doesn't come here quite often. Yah. I only see him on Tuesdays…He wasn't married to my mom…We're not that quite close. [He doesn't know about my child] because he would've said something a long time ago…He never talks to me. He never talks to me. He only talks to me if, 'Bring me a glass of water'. That's the only – he doesn't talk about – [pause] life.

Luthando: He's in Port Elizabeth. He doesn't know about this…he got disappointed with my mother when I was five years old. So, he has to pay support. Because he got married to another woman. He left me when I was five years, and then he got married to another woman. And then that other woman, he also has another son who is the same age as me…I don't know how it happened. Because – my brother, he was born only 21st September 1987. And I was born on the 16th September 1987.

Xolile: My father didn't change, because now he had another child to that woman that I told you about…so now it's hard for me. And to see my father is not even try to change. Because, he still see this woman, even now.

Sabier: My father – like that he didn't give me advice and – *naai* – we don't still talk…he wasn't in the house that time. He was *jolling*, man [having affairs]…He never talk with me, so I don't *mos* know what do he think.

The fourth category of fathering was that of the 'angry father' – the fathers who, while present, only had angry words for their sons, and who shouted and criticised without guiding or loving. Dumisani's account of his father was indicative of probably about one-third of the young men's experiences:

Dumisani: The stress was for that – my father is over-strict, you see [pause]. He always advised all his children; like having a child it is not something he liked. My dad liked that a person should complete schooling first and have certain things [pause] then one can have a child. I was scared of things like that [pause] and I was thinking [pause] how am I going to face him. He has always said that he doesn't want such things to happen [pause] but I broke his rules and that is what stressed me a lot…My dad saw me as a wrong person after having the baby…He didn't show any support [pause]. He took me as a person who has fumbled big time. I was a bad person during that time. Now he's not the same as before. At that time he didn't even want the baby to come to my home when it's born.

For Dumisani and others, an overly strict father was one who showed no support, seldom engaged in dialogue, did lots of 'shouting' and 'lecturing', and occasionally 'beat' their adult sons to underscore their disapproval and anger.

The final and fifth category was the father young men described as strict but loving, who spoke to, advised and guided them – whether living in the household or not. These were the 'talking fathers' (or 'caring' or 'friendly' fathers). Onathi's and Sakhile's relationships with their respective fathers illustrate two of the best examples of what it means to have a 'talking' father and how it affects the young men's own fathering practices. At the time of the study Onathi was living with his father (who was tragically shot and killed in the final stages of the study), although his mother lived nearby and he saw her regularly. He had just become a father and his son was under a year old. He was involved in an exclusive relationship with the mother of his child and was completing his matric through an FET college.

Onathi: My father has been the most helpful in helping me to be a good father. Because my father, like, he's the one who raised me up, so he taught me a lot of things in life. What to do. And when things happens, like, everything I must do. So, he taught me all the things, so I learnt from him – he's my role model, so. He's like my friend, so *we talk about everything*…I'm grateful with my father for doing that for me [talking and advising]…The advice he gave me – that I must find a job on weekends. On weekends I mustn't just stay at home, do nothing, yah. During the week I must go to school. He doesn't want me to drop out of school.

Sakhile: My father was a bit strict but at the end he gave me some advices. He said that I have rushed to do this but I shouldn't feel bad and all that. Everything will be alright because we also know the baby and we know Dee's family and the kind of people they are. [My father] has helped me [pause]. The way I was brought up. I've never seen my father shouting my mom…I would say I've learnt from him.

Sakhile raised the point that a 'talking' father can be both strict and loving. Tapelo spoke about how a good father 'mustn't shout at his child and at [the] time his child wants him, he must be there and must talk with his child'. This is a good summary not only of many of these young men's fathering aspirations, but also of the best of the fathering practices they experienced. When asked whether that was the kind of relationship he had enjoyed with his own father, Tapelo's response mirrored that of many others when he said his father had not been a 'talking father' largely due to the fact that he 'grew up in the old times':

Tapelo: No, my father wasn't like that, because he is an old person and he can't share everything. So I needed to talk to my mom about things. The problem is that my father grew up in the old times, so he is scared to talk about some other things.

Of course, some young men's fathers fit multiple categories. For example, most of the talking fathers were also financially supportive, but their key identifying feature for their sons was the fact that they engaged in dialogue with them rather than merely providing financially or only 'shout[ing] at them' in a one-way tirade. As rudimentary as this analysis is of young fathers' experiences of being fathered, it does provide a slate against which to evaluate these young fathers' own perceptions of what it *means* to be a good father and what it *takes* to be a good father. These two aspects will be explored in the remainder of this chapter.

What it means to be a good father

Although young men spoke quite animatedly (and unsolicitedly) about their relationships with their own fathers, it was in asking them about what makes someone a good father that their descriptions came alive. For almost all of the young men, being a good father revolved around being present and supporting their child, irrespective of whether they had an ongoing relationship with the mother of their child. But the meaning of good fathering also went much deeper than money and presence. Two young men's descriptions (Dumisani and Vuyo) highlight some of these nuances and are provided here, although there was a wealth of data from which to choose.

'Being a good man' and 'doing good things'

Dumisani, a young man from Umkomaas in KwaZulu-Natal who, at the time of the study, lived in a student residence in Mayville, became a father at 19 while still in matric. His child was looked after by the child's mother and grandmother and he hadn't 'spent a lot of time with him', only seeing his child during university holidays. He was not in a relationship with the mother of his child. His description of what it means to be a good father focused on both the kind of *character* a father should have and the *roles* that he should play in his child's life. It reflects both his current practice and some of his future desires for involvement with his child:

Dumisani: I think I would like him to remember me as being a father who was playing with him [pause]. His father who makes him happy, loves him a lot and who carries him – that's for now. But when he has maybe grown up and he is able to remember things [I hope] he will remember me as [a] hero, who can take care of things. Who doesn't give up when he's facing challenges…and – [pause]. It's that his father had good wishes for him.

The notion of being a hero to your child was repeated in at least five of these young fathers' answers, with at least three more saying they wanted to be a role model to their children. Dumisani continued by describing the role that a good father ought to play as being one of advising, guiding, praising and supporting (with problems rather than only financially), as well as showing love:

Dumisani: He must be able to advise his children when they are wrong [pause] and if they are doing alright he must also praise them. He must also support them when they have problems even if he can't solve them for them. He must show the love to them and say, 'I would have loved to do that but because of certain challenges I couldn't [pause]'. You should set rules as a father, but not rules that causes stress on the child and [makes him] even think of committing suicide [pause]. I think wherever he is [pause] he must not think about having other women on the side. I think he should think more of the mother of his child and his child.

His last comment of how a good father should be in a committed relationship with the mother of his child, while not true of his scenario, points to the fact that Dumisani, like others, strongly believes that being in a committed relationship with the mother of their children is first prize.

Time, physical affection and practical involvement

Vuyo, a young man from Langa, became a father at the age of 15 and, at the time of the study, was completing Grade 10 at school. He was in a relationship with the mother of his child at the time the child was born, but that ended. His description of what it takes to be a good father began by speaking of the fact that even if you are unable to support the child financially (due to being at school or unemployed), providing the child with love and being involved in their everyday care is key:

Vuyo: Even if you are in school, if you want to be a perfect father, you will do it. Because if you give love to your child – the important thing is love. [Financial] support too, but love is important…I'm not staying with my child, but [pause] – mmm, I make sure I see her. I see my child almost every day…Like I sacrifice everything for her, to show I love her. Yes. I sacrifice everything. If Nee [my child] is sick, I know I can't drink. Ah, every time I have her next to me. I go with my child, maybe going to church. Then we go to my friends, then the whole day I sit with her. Play with her, with my friends. Change her Pampers [nappy] [laughs].

Vuyo, like many of the other young men, spoke at length of being involved as much as possible in his child's day-to-day care, changing nappies, bathing her, and being around at supper time to sit with her and feed her. This was not an unusual practice, especially for the young men who lived in close proximity to their children – whether or not they were in a relationship with the mother of their child. Like Dumisani, Vuyo reflected on what would be important in order to be a 'perfect father':

Vuyo: To live with my child and the mother of my child [and to] have my own family…because I think then I'm gonna be a perfect father. Then give my kids love, everything. Everything my kids want. If I can [make] a plan to give her everything…and love – I think it will make me to be a good father to her. Yes.

Luthando, a young man who lives in the same area in Langa and who is involved with the mother of his child (but with whom he does not live), elaborated by saying that you should show your child physical affection. If he sees his child is crying or upset, 'I just take her and hug her'. He wants his child to grow up knowing him as 'someone who understands. Someone whose heart is warm, *neh?*'

The things a father should not do

Two young men provided good examples of behaviour that prevents someone from being classified as a good father. Lungile and Sakhile are both from Durban and each is in a relationship with the mother of his child (although not exclusive). They are also both geographically separated from their children and share views on what a good father should *not* do:

Lungile: [A child's] home has to have a straight rules and the father should be respectable [pause]. He must have dignity [pause] that's a good father. I would tell him [my child] that [pause] he mustn't drink because I don't drink too. When he stays with me I don't want to continue drinking [pause] and let him see what kind of a person am I [pause]. I want to stop drinking alcohol and tell him [pause] that I don't drink. He will see the good things I do [pause] so that when he has his own children he's able to tell them about how his father has brought him up. At the moment I'm not [a] good one [father] – yah, but when he is with me [pause] I'll change everything that I do and do the right things. I will stop drinking [pause] and know that the money I get is for my child.

Sakhile: I think it's caring [pause]. He has to take care of his children…[Someone] who is able to talk to his children; not a father who is shouting and beating his children all the time and being angry all the time. Even when a child is joking with him, he just tell the child to fuck off… He must talk to the child and give advice…I don't like to be like those fathers who [pause] are troublesome. I would talk to my child if she has made a mistake – I won't beat her. A good father should always be friendly. Don't be a father who is always shouting [at] the child's mother [pause]. Maybe they are always arguing – that is not needed. And also doing inappropriate things in front of the kids like drinking alcohol, that should be avoided.

Being respectable was equated with not drinking or swearing in front of children, not being angry and not shouting or beating your children. Lwandile added that a good father should have a 'good reputation in the community'.

Being there and providing financially

The final characteristics of a good father included 'being there' and 'working for the child'. Nearly all the young men spoke of these two facets of fatherhood in various ways, as evidenced in the examples of Ibrahiem, an unemployed young man from Bonteheuwel who became a father at 18 and who, at the time of the study, was in an exclusive relationship with the mother of his child; and Lwethu, an unemployed young man from Langa who spent a lot of time with his child, despite not being in a relationship with the child's mother:

Ibrahiem: I don't feel like a real father because I'm not working. I'm not supporting and that. *A father's job is to be there and support his family* and I'm not doing that and that's what makes me feel a bit down…I must stand by her [my child]…He's there to help the child. There when his child is maybe, like, feeling sad or something. He must talk with him if he wants advice. He should give him advice…he doesn't give the child bad advice. Maybe he gives good advice – and puts her on the right – shows her the right path and that's a good father.

Lwethu: What will make me a good father is if I have a child with a person that I'm sure that I'm committed with – [that] I'm gonna spend the rest of my life with. Cos it's not gonna be a very good thing for my child to see me with another girl leaving her mother hurt…[and] you can show your love, you see? Don't be afraid. Like, every once in a while, I tell her, 'I love you', even though she can't talk or anything. Every once in a while I tell her, 'I love you.' Show your affection, hug her, you see? Make sure you see her. Make sure that she has everything a child needs, you see? Everything a child should have, you see? Not spoil her, but make sure she has everything she needs, not everything she wants, you see?…I give money to Kee. 'Here's some money, do this and do that. For everything that's short.' You see? If I earn R500, I give her R200 – it's like that.

Both Ibrahiem and Lwethu began by talking about providing support, but then continued to describe the importance of being physically present in the lives of their children. Clearly, it was the combination of 'being there' and 'providing' that was ideal. And if you were present, provided financially, talked to your child, and provided love, care and were playful – that was the best of all. Fadiel, the young man from Bonteheuwel who has two same-aged children from two different young women, and Siya, the young man who became a father at 14 and dropped out of school for a year to support the child before returning, have the final words on this matter of support and presence:

Fadiel: A good father – someone that provided for them, that showed them the right way, that gave them something when they ask for it and someone for them to talk to. A good father speaks to his children and shows them the right way. He tells them when they are doing wrong and protects them from the wrong things. He does everything to provide for his children.

Siya: Basically what makes someone a good father is not support. Yah, it's not financial support! Because you can give your child financial support, but the child you will find she is very vulnerable with men because there was not a father figure in her life before! So, um, to be a father to me is to be there for a child when she needs you and be that father figure for her. Um, she must not go outside and find that father figure because that is where they get sugar daddies and other kind of stuff!

In thinking through young men's descriptions of the meaning of good fathering, it is striking to note that while being able to provide financial support was important to nearly all of them, it was the other characteristics that they appreciated in their own fathers (or regretted most not having) and wanted to provide for their children. So being a 'hero', playing with your child, being involved in daily activities (such as changing nappies, which does not fit the usual 'black' male stereotype), and living with and caring for your child epitomised good fathering in these young men's opinions. This is an interesting (and somewhat surprising) observation, as we turn to the final consideration in this chapter – that of teasing out what it *takes* to be a good father.

What it takes to be a good father

Almost overwhelmingly, these 27 young men spoke of the need to be employed and able to provide money as the most important means for them to ultimately be a good father. Table 4.2 provides the

TABLE 4.2   *Young fathers' journey through school to finding employment*

Young father	Status prior to child	Status after child born	Status in 2008	Hoped-for future status
Langa young men				
Andile	School	School	School	Work
Jabu	School	Worked for two years	School	Musician
Lonwabo	Dropped out of school	Unemployed	Unemployed[a]	Work
Luthando	School	School (failed matric)	Employed	Work – better job
Luxolo	School	School (finished)	Employed	Work – better job
Lwandile	School	School	School	Study – lawyer
Lwethu	School	School (completed)	Unemployed	Work
Ntombisa	School	Dropped out of school	Unemployed	Work
Onathi	School	School	School	Study
Saki	School	School	Studying	Work – business
Siya	School	Worked for a year	School	Study
Tapelo	School	School (dropped out)	Unemployed[a]	Work – trade
Vuyo	School	School	School	Work
Xolile	School	School	Unemployed	Work
Bonteheuwel young men				
Fadiel	Dropped out of school	Unemployed	Unemployed	Work – trade
Ibrahiem	School	Dropped out of school	Unemployed	Work – trade
Marlin	School	Dropped out of school	Unemployed	Work – trade
Sabier	Expelled from school	Unemployed	Unemployed	Work – trade
Yusuf	School	Dropped out of school	Employed	Work – trade
Zaid	Dropped out of school	Returned to school	Employed	Work
Durban young men				
Bongani	School	School	School	Study
Dumisani	School	School	Studying	Work – professional
Lungile	School	Dropped out of school	Unemployed	Work
Nhlanhla	School	School	Self-employed	Work – mechanical
S'bu	School	School (failed matric)	Unemployed	Work
Sakhile	School	School	Studying	Work – professional
Sifiso	School	School	Studying	Work – professional

Note: a Lonwabo and Tabelo had sporadic casual employment, but were mainly unemployed.

trajectory through which each passed from their status prior to becoming a father, how it changed (if it did) once their baby was born, what their current status is and what their hoped-for future status is. The trends are not difficult to discern. Seven young men dropped out of school once their babies were born to 'go and work for the baby', although two (Siya and Jabu) returned (after one and two years respectively). Tapelo dropped out of school three years after his baby was born because he had a drinking problem and would frequently come to school intoxicated. His dropping out was not an intentional choice to go and work in order to support his child.

A number of young men had already dropped out of school by the time they became fathers (Lonwabo, Zaid, Sabier, Fadiel) – becoming fathers had nothing to do with their dropping out. However, as can be seen from Table 4.2, all of the latter, with the exception of Zaid, remain unemployed. Zaid, in fact, returned to school after his baby was born, encouraged by the child's arrival to complete school in order to 'get a better job – to provide for my child'. For the rest of these young men, having a child did not interrupt their schooling. In spite of these various relationships between schooling and work, young men were unanimous when asked what most hindered their ability to be good fathers. Answers centred on money and employment in almost all cases. Young men either wanted to be employed or, if they were already employed, wanted a better job in order to provide for their child. *Working* was what it took to be a good father in their minds.

Work and money as the main criteria for fatherhood

Dumisani became a father at 19 while still in school and at the time of this project was still studying. In his account of what it takes to be a father he lamented his inability to support his child but added that he could still give 'love to a child'. He and Siya are alone when they contrast what it *takes* to be a good father (employment and money) with what it *means* to be a good father (emotionally present and engaged). For the rest of the young fathers in this study, being able to provide financially assumed priority status:

Xolile: I cannot say that I'm a perfect father, because I'm not working.

Luthando: I'm not a perfect father, cos I don't have money.

Lungile: I'm happy in a way, but there is nothing to be happy about because I'm not doing anything for her. At least if I had certain income; I would be happy if I was doing something.

S'bu: I'm not feeling alright at the moment, because I'm not working, and since I'm unable to give that support.

Sifiso: Being a father [pause] I can say being a father makes me happy, because it feels great to know I can also bring someone on earth. But it's better to be a father when you are responsible enough, maybe have a source of income.

Nhlanhla: It's really hard to be a young father, especially when you don't have income of your own.

Many spoke of how their self-esteem was hurt by being unemployed, still in school or studying, and so being unable to provide for their child:

Ibrahiem: What I remember is just – I wanted to find work. I wanted to work for her [my child]…I don't work at the moment. Then they [her family] say: 'You can't even buy [things for] the child.'

And all of that. That's what makes me feel down, feel a little junk. [My child's] mother just sits there and laughs if they talk to me like that.

Luthando: I don't feel nice…I'm a father. I can't – I can't do everything for my daughter. So, I just feel like a kid. I – I just feel small, because – I can't look after my baby, you see?…Other people are looking after her. My mother is looking after the baby. And then her parents look after the baby. So, I feel small. I don't feel nice.

This was exacerbated by having to depend on parents to support the child, even when one was already a 'man', i.e. had undergone the circumcision rite of *ulwaluko* (in amaXhosa culture), as in the case of Onathi:

Onathi: What I want is like – what I really want, when I'm finished studying, like I want to get a job, like nice job, so I can get – I can get the money. So I can stop depending on my parents. And I hate the depending on them. I'm a man now. A man's supposed to stand on their own. But I'm not working yet, but I'm still schooling, yah.

Vuyo: I give her, eh, R400 a month…It's my father's money.

Sabier: I don't like to depend, man. That's why I'm gonna go work.

For many young men, their parents were materially involved in supporting their child, and while they were grateful, it also made them feel inadequate or, as Luthando described, 'I feel small'. A number of young men who depended on parents to support their child showed enormous enterprise in finding 'piecework' or casual jobs. For example, Nhlanhla became self-employed by starting a mechanical workshop in the township in which he lived in order to support his child:

Nhlanhla: I work for myself. I have a workshop [pause]. A mechanical workshop here in Bonella. I have place which I use for work. So when I had child, I was 18 turning 19 years old…and I saw that I should make means so that he can grow – being responsible.

Others, such as Andile, Onathi (see earlier), Sifiso and Siya, worked casual jobs in order to support their child while they were still at school:

Andile: I feel good. I'm able to support sometimes…I am doing some work. I wash the dishes [at the] taxi rank. I work for a woman who sells food for taxi drivers.

Sifiso: But I persevered. I did my matric and I passed it. So I did piece jobs in order to be able to support my child and my parents supported me and my child, until now.

Siya: Um, my father gives me. My father owns a funeral parlour so, um, on Saturdays and Sundays I do funerals for him.

Staying in school or dropping out to go and work

Seven young men dropped out of school, either completely or for a period, in order to work for their children. Yusuf, Jabu and Siya described these circumstances:

Yusuf: I told her that it's fine, she can finish her schooling and I will go and look for a job. And that's what I did. I worked for the whole year. The baby wasn't even born yet and she had everything, nappies and all.

Jabu: It was like destroying me because I had to leave school. Because I had to – I had to find something to get some money…I was two years [out of school working for baby, then went back to school].

Siya: So the year that I was not at school, I was suppose to go and find work. At first I was just working as an assistant in a cash store – I was permanent for that year.

For the young men who stayed in school, their reasoning was that by staying in school they would ultimately secure a better future for their children, and be able to move on to tertiary studies or 'proper jobs' rather than becoming 'a grass cutter'. Onathi's father asked him what he wanted to do and his reply was, 'I don't want to work and get a low-pay work…I still want to go to school.' Andile's family (he was looked after by his grandfather and uncle) agreed to support his child while he continued at school; the payment they wanted in return was that he:

Andile: 'Provide for the child when you are working.' That's what they need in return! So they want from me to be a good father. A good father when I am working! But now they are making me a good father by supporting [my child] by themselves!

Siya described how, after he and the mother of his child had initially both dropped out of school, the best option was for them to leave the child with her parents while they completed their schooling and 'build futures for ourselves so that he may benefit from that…to create a better future for him'. This decision, to leave the raising of their child to either her or his parents (not an infrequent occurrence among this group), was not without cost. Sifiso spoke of the pain his decision to continue with his studies brought:

Sifiso: We are not that close…I don't stay with her [my child]…It hurts, but there is nothing I can do because [pause] I also have things to do here.

As already alluded to in Chapter 3, money was a major cause for young men denying paternity. Luxolo described how he spent the first three months of his child's life ignoring both his daughter and her mother due to the stress of needing to pay support, while Lwethu described how being poor (and having to contend with damages payments) exacerbated this stress and the consequent temptation to run away:

Luxolo: So for three months I just ignored my child and her mother. And if I saw them coming in front, I just take another way. Because I don't want to see them…Because we're gonna talk about this [money]…Where will I get the money, you see – [I was] stressing – [about how] to support the child.

Lwethu: The problem is with people – it's just that fathers – they're afraid that they're not going to be able to support financially. So, they decide, 'No, no, no, no, this is not mine', because they are running away from payments. It's okay with white-collared [workers], they say, 'No, this is my baby', you see? They always support, but us blacks, it's that thing with paying the stomach [damages] and you have to support. You have to, you see?

However, despite young men's vociferous talk about the relationship between working and being a good father, the relationship between employment, unemployment and the studying status of young fathers and the nature of their relationship with the mother of their child proved complex (see Table 4.3). Of the seven young men who were employed at the time of the study, three were together with the mother of their child in a committed relationship while four were not. Of the 11 respondents who were studying in a tertiary institution or who were still at school, four were in a relationship with the mother of their child while seven were not.

TABLE 4.3 *The link between young fathers' employment/studying status and their relationship with the mother of their child*

Name	Relationship status (2008)
Employed	
Luthando	Together
Luxolo	Not together
Nhlanhla	Together
Yusuf	Not together
Zaid	Together
Schooling/Studying	
Andile	Together
Bongani	Not together
Dumisani	Not together
Jabu	Not together
Lwandile	Not together
Onathi	Together
Saki	Not together
Sifiso	Not together
Siya	Together
Vuyo	Not together
Sakhile	Together
Unemployed	
Fadiel	Together/Not together*
Ibrahiem	Together
Lonwabo[a]	Not together
Lungile	Together (not exclusive)
Lwethu	Not together (casual)
Marlin	Together

(continued)

Name	Relationship status (2008)
Ntombisa	Not together
S'bu	Together
Sabier	Together
Tapelo[a]	Not together
Xolile	Together (not exclusive)

Note: *Fadiel has two children, each with a different woman.

    a Lonwabo and Tapelo had sporadic casual employment, but were mainly unemployed.

Finally, of the eleven young men who were unemployed, seven were in a relationship with the mother of their child (all but one in an exclusive relationship) while four were not with the mother of their child.

This is interesting given the high value placed on employment in young men's descriptions of what it takes to be a good father. Among the group of young fathers in this study, more who were unemployed remained in a committed and exclusive relationship with the mother of their child than those who were employed. Among this study group, educational status rather than employment seems to be a better indicator of whether a young father remains in a relationship with the mother of his child after the birth of the child. Twice as many young fathers who were still in school or studying at the time their baby was conceived, compared with those who were either employed or unemployed, tended to no longer be in a relationship with the mother of their child some time after the birth of the child.

Conclusion

This chapter has highlighted three main issues in the phenomenology of young fatherhood in South Africa. The first is that although many young fathers themselves grow up in 'absent father' families, many use this adversity as motivation for being intentionally present to their own children. While the literature shows that growing up in a failed fathering environment predicts adverse outcomes for young men, including early fatherhood (Gohel et al. 1997), it appears silent on how failed fathering experiences provide motivation to young fathers. This is an important finding of this study.

Second, despite the stereotypes to the contrary, these young 'black' (and 'coloured') fathers from impoverished communities have not absented themselves from the lives of their children even if they are no longer romantically involved with the mother of their child. In this regard, the literature paints contrasting portraits. On the one hand, it confirms these findings in numerous studies which show young fathers to be involved in the emotional and physical care of their children. Glikman (2004) found that young, low-income African American fathers were significantly involved in the lives of their children one year after the inception of the study. Hollander (1996), in a study of 307 African American young women in Maryland, USA, found that although young men frequently do not provide financial support, a significant number – including those no longer in a relationship with the MOC – were participating in childcare responsibilities. However, other studies show how teen fathers tend to 'vanish' over time: within five years in an Australian study (Colman 1993) and in a US study, up to two-thirds of young fathers do so within three years (Kalil et al. 2005). As a snapshot rather than a longitudinal study, this investigation can neither confirm nor deny this latter picture of young fathers.

The third conclusion of this chapter centres on the strange anomaly that exists between what impoverished young fathers have identified as important in their own experience of being fathered and what they believe they need to do in order to be a good father – what we have called the difference between what it *means* to be a good father and what it *takes* to be a good father. On the one hand, young fathers appreciate Morrell's (2006: 18) assertion that 'the position of a father cannot be measured simplistically in terms of his physical absence or presence…A father might well be physically present, but emotionally absent, or physically absent but emotionally supportive', and they applaud the emotional presence that their fathers gave them (or rue his emotional absence). At the same time, however, they place enormous store on their own *financial* presence in the lives of their children and elevate it to the most important feature of fatherhood, with tragic consequences since their poverty and unemployment militates against sustained financial involvement. In this respect, the literature suggests that teen fathers who are more involved with their own fathers place greater store on the provider or breadwinner role of fathers than those who grew up without present fathers (Broadfield 2006; Bucklin 1999; Edwards et al. 1986), while other studies show that an appreciation of the emotional presence (or 'recreational' role) of a father is a more recent phenomenon characteristic of modernist (or postmodernist) societies rather than of traditional societies (Milkie et al. 1997).

An explanation of young men's presence despite their poverty, and the centrality of financial responsibility, are themes that form the central tenets of Chapter 5, which explores the role that the young father's mother, the mother of his child and her family, as well as cultural expectations play in hindering or enabling young men's involvement with their children.

CHAPTER 5

Mothers, damages and 'her family': Influences, practices and relationships in the life of a young father

In setting the research priorities for this study, it was decided that a key feature must be to identify those factors which *hinder* a young father from fully participating in the life of his child, and those factors that *enable* a young man to do so. In the preceding chapter, among other issues raised, the central role of employment for young fathers was repeatedly referred to by participants. Being able to provide for a child was key in a young father's decision to remain involved with his child, feel good about himself and also strive to improve his ability to support the child in the future by completing schooling or tertiary studies.

In this chapter, three main features are considered as further forces operating on young fathers' lives. Unlike Chapter 4, which considered at length the role of their own fathers in young men's conceptions of what it means to be a good father, this chapter focuses on the powerful influence that young men's *mothers* have on them. Second, it considers some of the traditional practices (especially for the young amaXhosa and amaZulu fathers) which include, but are not limited to, money. Finally, it documents young fathers' perceptions and experiences of how the mother of their child's family hinders or helps them in their quest to be good fathers.

To begin, however, it is interesting to note all the factors that these young fathers directly identified as most and least helpful. Young men were asked to write down the names of three people or things which they found most helpful in their efforts to be a good father and those they found least helpful. Twenty-four[18] young men identified 71 most helpful features and 64 least helpful factors. Figure 5.1 on page 57 provides two examples of young men's most and least helpful lists. Zaid's list highlights the dichotomy between his and the MOC's family's perceived support. Lwethu's list details other factors helping and hindering young fathers' involvement with their children: mothers, school and community as helpful, and alcohol, multiple partners and not being in a steady relationship as hindering factors.

Table 5.1 on page 58 tabulates these 'most and least helpful' lists for all research participants and includes the number of times each factor was mentioned.

The results show that for the majority of young men it is *their* family members who provide the most support, encouragement and motivation to be or to become a good father. Figure 5.2 on page 59 provides two examples of young fathers' 'three field maps', representing the people involved in 'the story of me and my baby' and the degree of closeness of each. Sifiso's representation shares much in com-

---

18 Two young men did not complete the activity, because they did not participate in a second interview, while one young man arrived a day early for his interview, before this activity had been finalised.

FIGURE 5.1 *Two young fathers' 'most and least helpful' priority lists*

People/things	MOST helpful	People/Things	LEAST helpful
my mom	1	her mom	1
my sister	2	her dad	2
my uncle	3	her auntie	3

People/Things	MOST helpful	People/Things	LEAST helpful
Mother	1	Alcohol	1
School	2	Having too many girlfriends	2
Community	3	Not being in a steady, Permanent Relationship	3

Sources: Top: Zaid, 18, Bonteheuwel, Western Cape; Bottom: Lwethu, 19, Langa, Western Cape

mon with the other young men in the study, who focus on their own social networks in this diagram, i.e. 'my sister', 'my mother', 'my father', 'my granny' and 'my friends'. In Zaid's map, while 'my mom', 'my grandma' and 'my grandpa' are also evident, certain members of the MOC's family are also depicted, although at a greater distance from the closer, more intimate circle. For example, 'my gf's [girlfriend's] mom' is depicted on the edge of the second circle, while 'my gf's dad' is on the edge of the outermost circle. So, while a few, like Zaid, do include members of the mother of their child's family in their circles, they position them at a distance from close involvement.

In the least helpful list (Table 5.1), young men mainly listed unemployment and a lack of money as the biggest hindrance to them in their quest to be a good father. Most had stories of members of their own extended family who had said or done something hurtful, and they were also quick to point out a general lack of relationship with the family of their child's mother. This was, as expected, acute in

TABLE 5.1   *Young fathers' 'most helpful, least helpful' priority list*

Most helpful person or thing	No. of times listed	Least helpful person or thing	No. of times listed
Own mother	15	Unemployment or a lack of money	10
Fathers (including two who mentioned their father's absence as a helpful factor)	10	Extended family members (grandmothers, grandfathers, uncles, aunts, cousins)	9
Extended family, especially uncles (4), but including grandmothers (3), cousins (1) and aunts (1)	9	Mother of child's family (especially father and male family members but also mother and aunt)	8
Siblings	8	Consuming alcohol (and being involved in violence)	6
Friends	6	No steady relationship with mother of child	4
Seeing other fathers or reading books or watching media about fatherhood	5	Siblings	4
Community or school support	5	Geographical separation from child or denying the child	4
Making right choices, avoiding alcohol and having a sense of dignity	4	Being too young	3
Mother of child's female family members (sister, mother, grandmother, aunt)	4	Incomplete schooling or studies	3
Spending time with their child	3	Having other girlfriends	3
Mother of child	1	Friends	3
Getting married	1	Community and culture	3
Current girlfriend who is supportive	1	Fathers	2
Completing schooling or studies	1	Selfishness, stress and depression	2

cases where they no longer had a relationship with the mother of their child. Young men's alienation from the families of the mother of their child was corroborated in their 'three field maps'. Almost no young father included people outside of their immediate family and friendship circle. In other words, they didn't include members of the mother of their child's family or wider community influences such as schoolteachers, neighbours, clinics, or church or traditional leaders.

The role of young fathers' mothers

The role of mothers in impoverished communities has been repeatedly documented as that of 'the strong black female' (Mirza 1993: 38). The portrayals of these young fathers' relationships with their mothers are no different. Mothers are depicted in four main roles: as provider, as emotional supporter and encourager, as mediator and protector, and as counsellor or teacher. Lwethu captured all these roles when speaking of the most helpful people in young fathers' lives:

FIGURE 5.2 *Two young fathers' 'three field maps'*

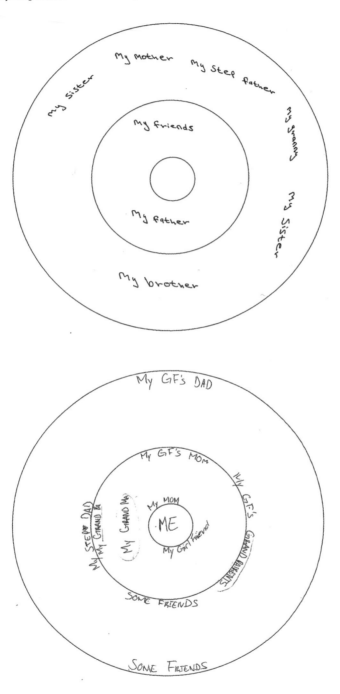

Sources: Top: Sifiso, 23, Bonella, KwaZulu-Natal; Bottom: Zaid, 18, Bonteheuwel, Western Cape

Lwethu: My mother was the first one to know, before her mother. My mother was the first one to know, because my mother is kind of *cool*, you see. She's not old-fashioned…

It's cos if a mother has been always by your side, you see, [in] everything. Cos sometimes I take time to think. You think, man, of all the things she's done for you during the years, and everything. Cos my mother, there was a time that she was not working, but I didn't see that. I had full uniform, everything, when I went to school. Every time there was an outing, she made sure that I had money to go, you see? All those things, all those things, you see? Makes you realise how important your mother is…

I consider my mom to be a good father and a good mother, you see?…She *taught* me, and from the way she brought me up, you see?…she *advises* me, everything, yah. My – I'm not that close with my father, cos I never had time, you see, to bond with him. You see? Cos everything, even things concerning men, I *talk* with my mother cos she's the *calm* one. She's more calm about it…So, my mom helped me to be a better father…

I really, like, really, really *love* my mom, so I don't want to do anything to hurt her…

I have to keep a very good reputation so that some things can't go to my mother, cos everything goes around, goes around, goes around and comes to my mother…I'm not afraid she'll throw me out of the house [but] I'm very afraid cos she gets *hurt* very easily, so I'm *afraid of disappointing* her, you see?

She only shouts at me because I'm unemployed and sitting, doing *loxion* management [am unemployed].

Lwethu speaks of his mother as a provider who, despite being unemployed at one stage, ensured he had everything he needed for school. He speaks of her as emotional supporter and encourager, the one who is calm, who talks with him, and tells that she was 'the first one to know' about his imminent fatherhood. He also speaks of how his mother advises him, acts as mediator and protector, and as counsellor or teacher. Finally, he speaks of how he is careful to protect his reputation since he doesn't want to hurt his mother, and explains that the only time his mother acts as a disciplinarian is when he's not looking for work. These latter themes, of mother as emotional supporter, counsellor and teacher, were repeatedly flagged by the young men in this study:

Onathi: Who has helped me to be a perfect father? Like, I can say my mother. Because she's the one who really understands me. She's the one that put all her time to the baby…like she's doing all the work…She's giving me hope that – like, I could be the person that I want. Like being a perfect father, yah. [That I] mustn't lose hope about my baby. She's there for me.

Marlin: Be strong and believe, and think about your mother who is always there for you, because your mother will cover up. With certain things, your father will tell your mother, 'Wait. You shouldn't step in. He must learn.' But your mother will step in for you.

Jabu: Because you see when you grow up with your mother, and your mother tell you the things, you know, that you one day when you have the family, you must be present for your baby. And support, uh, you know, and be a responsible man.

S'bu: She told me that I have to be educated, complete my matric and go to tertiary, because it won't help to be in a rush to work while I don't have a certificate.

Luthando: My mother told me that I should stick with my girlfriend.

Sabier: My mommy. She just told me like now I must – I was in the drugs so she told me I must stop that.

Zaid: I think my mother because – and I said she never used to talk about sex to me or stuff like that, but when the day that I told her I'm preg- – Bee's pregnant, and I gave her the pregnancy test [pause], then she started talking more after that to me. Like serious stuff about the relationship and stuff like that.

But Lwethu, like many of the other young fathers in this study, also alluded to some of the roles that his mother *doesn't* play in his life when he said 'she only shouts' because he's unemployed. In mediating for them, especially with their fathers or the MOC's family, or taking on too much responsibility for the care and support of their child, mothers may actually be failing to teach their sons responsibility, courage and independence. Saki is one such case:

Saki: [My mother] was always there for me. She said that she wants what is best for my son. And she will take the son as if he was her son. [So now] I'm taking my child as my brother…I felt that it was my mother's responsibility to do everything to my son…She made me believe that she'd take care of my son. I must focus on my studies. I must make something of myself. If I keep on telling myself that I have a responsibility that would have been a problem for me. I was very young then. I think what I've done is the best thing…It's not as if I will take my child away from my parents. It's just I will give my mother money to cover expenses.

Part of the consequence of Saki's mother taking complete responsibility for his son is that Saki now believes he will never take the child away from his parents and raise him as his son. Instead, he is content to regard him as a younger brother. Whether that is in the best long-term interest of the child is debatable. So, even though mothers are an important force in contributing to their sons' success as young fathers, it seems that in failing to play the role of disciplinarian (and in the absence of a father or father figure), mothers fail their sons.

In addition, young men seldom speak of how their mothers help them beyond providing emotional and financial support. Few impoverished mothers have the social capital or networks to play the role of facilitator – common in middle-class homes – where parents provide their children not only with emotional support, but also with the information, knowledge and skills to help them get a job, use condoms responsibly or curb damaging habits (especially around drugs and alcohol). In impoverished communities, mothers love and support their sons – yet they have the potential to do so much more, given the nature of their close relationship and the high regard in which young men in general, and these young fathers in particular, hold their mothers.

Young men's relationships with the child's mother and her family

As central and helpful as mothers are to these young fathers, the next highest category on the least helpful list that young men composed (after unemployment and a lack of money) comprises other family members,[19] the members of 'her family' and the young father's relationship with the mother of his child. Participants were especially explicit about the problems that 'her father', 'her uncles' and 'her brothers' gave them, and how these male members of the MOC's family frequently were the biggest hindrances to them fulfilling their role as young fathers.

Yusuf's and Lonwabo's accounts of their relationship with the mother of their child and her family provided perhaps the two saddest and most dramatic examples of how a young man is excluded from raising his child.[20] Lonwabo's story has already been referred to in Chapters 3 and 4. After dropping out of school in Grade 9 to pursue a calling to become a traditional healer, he became a father at the age of 18 in an alcohol-fuelled ('when maybe we were drunk then we did this thing – sleep together') casual relationship he had with one of his mother's patients (his mother was also a traditional healer). He was ecstatic to hear about the baby but his happiness soon turned to bitterness when first the MOC's family rejected him, and then the mother of his child announced to her family that he was in fact not the father – that the father was, in the words of Lonwabo, 'a rich guy [who] works for the government'. When the baby was born, Lonwabo frequently visited 'to change nappies or change the bathwater' until 'her father started pushing me away'. At times, the young woman furtively 'brings the baby to [my] home' but for the most part he is 'kicked out the door' as soon as he tries to visit.

At the time of the study, Lonwabo was 24 years old and unemployed. Three years ago he married the cousin of the mother of his child, who does not know about his child's existence. He is convinced he is the father of the child – and comments that people who see the child can see the resemblance between them. He openly admits he has a problem with alcohol, which he struggles to beat. So when her father calls him a 'drunkard', he feels this is justified. But he believes that it's not just his drinking that hinders his relationship with his child; it's also because 'that family is a high-class family of which I don't think they want anything to do with me…maybe I'm no good to them, from their lifestyle, you know. Maybe that's it.' However, his longing for his child and his wish 'to be a good father [in order to] give back…the things that I did not get' from his own father, and the way in which he reflects on his own fatherlessness ('longing for that father bond') and his desire to be there for his son, is very sad ('It's really hurting for me as I do want to be, *neh*, the father to the baby but I don't know how…because I've been pushed away'). Lonwabo relates that 'sometimes I do have dreams about the baby – like – it's like – he's longing for me but I can't [pause] get to him'. Finally, in his second interview Lonwabo spoke of how participating in the study made him very emotional:

Lonwabo: I even cried at night, like, thinking about it, you see?…The thing is, it's so hard like…when my friends ask where is your child? Well, like sometimes, I can say like, which child?…it's like, *neh*, being a father [but] like not being a father to a baby!…Cos now I am like, I dunno if I have a child or not!

19   This category is artificially high because almost all young men had had some negative experience with members of their extended family. In grouping together aunts, uncles, cousins and grandparents, this category becomes unrepresentatively high. In addition, the stories seemed to be particular to each context, whereas the male members of the MOC's family seemed to represent a more coherent group of people who were ongoing hindrances in the lives of young fathers – no matter what the relationship was between the young father and the mother of his child.

20   Discussing how young women treat them with regard to accessing their child was a key feature of the debriefing and consultation workshop. One young father noted: 'They [the mothers] don't believe in 50:50 when it comes to support [for the child] – no, it must be 80:20 – we must do all the support – they just sit [pause]. That's not right.' Another young father asked: 'So you know that sometimes we – our families – look after the child and not the girl right? So have you ever seen a father make it difficult for the mother to see the child? Never! So why do they make it so difficult for us to see our children – you must bring this, do this, come this time – or don't come [shakes his head]. What's wrong with them?'

Yusuf's story is similar, except that both the mother of his child and her family have pushed him away, not because of alcohol problems or because they are 'higher class', but because she found another partner. Yusuf, from Bonteheuwel, became a father when he was 16. On hearing the news that his girlfriend was pregnant, he decided to drop out of school and find a job in order to be able to support the baby ('I worked for the whole year. The baby wasn't even born yet and she had everything, nappies and all'). However, he described the beginning of his problems as being when he spoke to her family:

Yusuf: When they got to my house, we greeted each other and they asked me if I know that she is pregnant. I said yes…then her father said I – now I have to marry her. Then I said, 'No, I won't do that.'

Shortly afterwards, he 'heard that the ex-boyfriend is coming over a lot these days, so I told myself that let me find myself another girlfriend':

Yusuf: She said she doesn't want to be with me any more. Then every day I was with a different girl at school and we kiss each other in the passage…When the baby was born she didn't want anything to do with me and when she sees me in the street she says I'm rubbish because of what I did to her. I just swore her, at her.

The mother of his child ended up marrying the ex-boyfriend, and developed a *tik* addiction:

Yusuf: About the mother [of our child]…she's not working. She's doing *tik*. That's why the child doesn't live with her. Because she uses *tik*. That's why sometimes I just want to take her to court. Because it's not nice – look, I work. I work very hard. Now I give her money for the child and then her and her friends use the money on *tik*…Sometimes I give the money to the granny. If I don't find the granny, then I give it to her. She's the child's mother. She must care for the child. And then I started hearing – no – I just sent money, then it's not even two weeks, then they're looking for money again. I get two containers of milk for the month… Then it's not even the half of the month, then both containers have been used already. Because her brother is also on drugs. So she and her brother steal the milk, then they sell it. And then – OK, a pack of Kimbies is the same. Lasts half the month, sometimes less…it's not even two weeks, then the nappies are done. And it's R150 a pack. And here I'm buying for it to last half the month. Then they sell it.

For a reason unknown to Yusuf, her parents prevent him from seeing the child:

Yusuf: It makes me crazy man, [not being able to see my child]. Because – look, I – I sometimes see other girls with their boyfriends. They were pregnant. Then they're not together any more. They give the child to him. But she doesn't, she doesn't want to do that with me. I don't know why.

Occasionally, the grandmother brings the child to see him. It's always furtive but he makes sure the child has a fun day:

Yusuf: The last time I did take her to the park and play with her. Then she ride on the bikes. Stuff like that, man. Yah. I take her out. Then, then I take her to Spur. *Somma* [just] here by Vangate Mall and then we walk here in the Mall. There's like this rides for the children and I put her on that stuff and show her *lekka* [nice], man…That was the last time we two have fun together.

Yusuf lamented:

Yusuf: When they [his child and her grandparents] walk past our place then she [his daughter] says she wants to come in there. But when she asks, they just walk on by. [When I go visit] sometimes they don't answer the door for an entire week. When I come again the next week, then it's, 'She's not here'. Then I go again, then I can hear there are people in the house and so on.

He described his feelings poignantly:

Yusuf: I think I overcame a big accident me – being so young with my first baby…[but] now I look like the fool…I work at Sea Point [suburb]. I see young couples every day who still have their girls with them – white couples with their babies walking on the beach – the father pushing the pram and the mother shooting with the video camera…that's just nice.

Yusuf is desperate to have regular contact with his child and has thought about going to court to ensure his rights as a father, but keeps putting it off. His fear concerns the fact that although he is working and currently providing for the child, his contract might end:

Yusuf: I was there [at court] again. Then…[I thought] if I should take her to court – this is not a permanent job I have. It's a contract…then I can't tell the courts that I can contribute each month to see the child. And what if my contract ends?…Then I can't pay, then whose gonna pay? Then money goes higher and higher, then they don't want to give the child again.

Yusuf fears for his future relationship with his daughter:

Yusuf: She probably thinks about where I am, thinks that I probably don't want to see her. And that's wrong, man. I wouldn't like to be a father – that they do this to her and me for another two years. 'No,' they'll tell her, 'your daddy's dead.' Tomorrow she'll walk by me in the street and then she wants to know from me: 'Why you weren't there?'…Then she will ask me where I've been all this time. That's the time I will have to tell her the truth, how your mother's been with me…

           Because girl babies – like small girls, man. They grow up so fast. They – like my friend – she has a daughter. She's three now. But what that child can talk about: 'Yes, my daddy was here. He did bring me money. He did bring me toys.' And then the father may not come for another two months. 'He did bring no money. No toys. No clothes.' Like that man. It makes me heartsore. Yoh, to hear what she talks about already. Now what if she grows up and her father visits one day, then she will just tell him, 'No, go man. I don't want you here. I don't want your money.' And things like that…like now, hey – I never talk to anyone about my feelings. Only with you. As I'm sitting here, I feel like crying.

Yusuf's and Lonwabo's stories are shared by a number of other young fathers in this study. The usual catalyst is that the couple have a falling-out and the relationship becomes acrimonious, with the family of the child's mother reinforcing the estrangement in (assumed) support of their daughter. Frequently, parents decide that the young man is not good enough for their daughter and place pressure on her not to see him. For many of the young 'black' men, the cultural tradition of damage payments produces a further reason for why they become estranged from their children. It is to this feature of these young fathers' lives that we now turn.

Cultural practices as obstacles to young fathers' involvement with their children

Of the 21 'black' respondents in the study, all but two[21] had either paid damages, were in the process of paying or had made an arrangement[22] with the girl's family about when damages would be paid. For most, the amount varied between R2 500 and R5 000, although negotiations often started much higher, with some families demanding R10 000. In the following dialogue, Luthando describes what damages payment is for, whether he agrees with it, and his own plan to pay it off, while enjoying both access to his child and good relations with her family in the meantime:

Luthando: The mother of my girlfriend sent me a letter that the family of my girlfriend, her uncles and grandfathers – they want to meet me on the first. It's about the money. Stomach money…it's like *lobolo* thing, but it's not *lobolo*.

Interviewer: It's for when a girl is pregnant?

Luthando: Yah. And then, my stepfather and my uncle, we go there. And then they said they want R5 000 – and then we came back. My stepfather said to me that, no, that is bullshit because it's not like Ree was a virgin when she fall pregnant. She was not a virgin.

Interviewer: And what do you think of damages payment? Do you think it's fair that you have to pay that?

Luthando: Because I know it's our culture. I accept it, you see?

Interviewer: So you will pay it?

Luthando: My mother said so, that we must pay it. Yah, because it's our culture. It was so when we did that, damage somebody's daughter.

Interviewer: And what happens to that money?

Luthando: It goes to the family. It's a something like *lobolo*. Because when – if I broke up with my girlfriend, *neh* – and then go to meet another woman, she will stay with my baby. And then [when] she meet another man, and then that man will say that I can't pay so much *lobolo*. She's already broken, you see?

Interviewer: Have you paid the money already?

Luthando: I'm still paying it even now. If you know my salary…

---

21   Lwethu claims that the two families decided that there was no need for damages and instead each family would contribute equally to the maintenance of the child. ('They [her family] have to come and discuss what we have to pay… But it was never like that. They came and they negotiated that we gonna look after this side, and you're gonna do this and this [on your] side. So, it's gonna be 50/50…No need for payments. No damages. No damages.') In Saki's case, negotiations broke down because of a falling-out between the two families over money, and so his family never paid damages, which has exacerbated the estrangement.

22   Dumisani: 'At the moment that is still under preparations. It can happen maybe in the next year. I haven't paid the damages as yet. But I explained to her family that it would happen and they also accepted that because they could see the situation.'

Interviewer: And what's your relationship like with her family at the moment, seeing you haven't finished paying yet?

Luthando: So far so good. They speak to me. I go there…

Interviewer: Oh, okay. So it's not disrespectful, *ukudliwa* to speak to them before you have paid?

Luthando: No, it's – I did the damage, you see, to their daughter…[and] we agreed…that was why we were talking because I was open to them. I didn't show them funny face.

Interviewer: And what does it mean to have paid damages?

Luthando: The money that I'm paying now, I'm paying it for if I want her [my child] to come where I am – [so if] I go back to Port Elizabeth, *neh*, her family will not have a problem [that the child comes with me]…because I've paid. It's like *lobolo*.

While it was difficult to pick up the many nuances of damage payments, these young fathers made a number of points quite clear. Negotiations occurred between the men of each family. Some insisted that it was the duty of the father's family to go and see the mother's family; others insisted that the mother's family should send a delegation to see the men of the father's family. All the amaXhosa young men were clear that if the young father was still a boy (*inkwenkwe*) and not a man (not having undergone the *ulwaluko* or initiation rite of passage into manhood), then he was not part of the negotiations. Others disagreed about whether being a man automatically included you in the negotiations or not. Another key feature was how exactly it was established that a young man was the father of the child. He was never asked directly whether he had had sex with the girl, but rather if 'he knows her'. If he said he knew her, then it was settled. He was the father and was liable for damage payment or stomach money – *ukubhatala isisu* in isiXhosa – to pay for 'breaking the stomach'. Onathi described his experience in detail:

Onathi: [Her family] they come [to our place]. My grandfather ask me, 'Do you know her?' And I'm like, 'Yes, I do know her.' And he says, 'That settles it, then this is your child.' I was like, 'Why you didn't ask me is [it] my child, or what?' [But] all they ask, 'Do you know her?' And you just say, 'Yes.' That's it. It's your baby…Then I sit again and we talked again, and then negotiate on some things, money, all that stuff. Like, how much must be paid for the stomach, all that. It's called *isisu*. So you must pay for the mess you have made…My father… paid R5 000…He had no choice…Those are the rules. They were set there by elders. So they can't just break them down, yah. You must pay damages – maybe R4 000 or R5 000. Just understand – you still have to buy clothes, support, all the things. The family take the money…maybe they use it for the baby when he need something. I don't know. I don't know what they do with the money…it's not *lobolo*. If you wanted to marry the girl you must still pay *lobolo* and *lobolo* is more expensive.

In the absence of money for damage payments, there is hurt (as in the case of Sifiso) and financial hardship, as illustrated by Nhlanhla:

Sifiso: It hurts me because [pause] a child must use his/her father's surname; but [pause] because of certain reasons she/he is forced to use his/her mother's surname; because I haven't paid to her family [pause]. Like I haven't paid the damages. After I've paid all the damages then she will use my surname…Because that child [pause] is mine; like if you have a child he/she doesn't belong to her mother's family but belongs to my family.

Nhlanhla: I live with my child's mother. Like I recently went to pay the damages and stuff. But it's not easy being a father you know [pause]. It's not easy. There are difficult times, when there are no diapers and you are low on budget…they requested me to buy a cow and a goat [pause] just for the damages, it's expensive, my sister. Not to talk about the *lobolo*, yoh!… You know when was it a good time? When I came to pay. Everybody loved me, I was the boss.

Only one young man disagreed with the practice of damage payments:

Jabu: I was very afraid. You see, when you're like, you are 18, you're still – you're still young to them. Yes, and they were asking like how am I going to take care of it. How am I going to buy things for the baby, because I was still at school…[My uncles] did pay, but they didn't pay all the amount. My uncles – they said I need to take responsibility. And he said he's not gonna pay for school for me. He was cross…He took care of everything because *I didn't need to say much. Because I have nothing*…[but] I think it's bad, because what is it for? I don't know what is it for? I don't believe it. Yes, yes, because they say it is a custom – something that has to be done. I think it's bad…

They went to my uncle. He's the one who says the baby is mine. So – I was not sure. I was not allowed by her family…It was decided among the parents. My uncle and Nee's mother. Her father is absent…They didn't talk to me…They say that's how things are done. They can't discuss like this matter with *inkwenkwe* [a boy]. Only with the elders…Mmm, I was young. I didn't know what to do…*I had nothing to say to the matter*. I was fine with it, and the way they did it. *Because that's how they do things in our culture.*

Jabu's story reveals a number of problems with *isisu* and the process of negotiation. First, his fear and lack of money means that he 'has nothing to say' because 'I have nothing'. Second, although he is unsure about whether the child is his (he had sex with the young woman while at a party without using a condom but isn't sure that he was her only partner), he notes that the elder 'didn't talk to me'. Instead, 'it was decided among the parents'. In Jabu's case, where there was no relationship with the mother of the child and no clear proof that he is the father, such a practice can clearly misidentify the father of the child. Finally, he vacillates between thinking the custom is bad but being 'fine' with it 'because that's how they do things in our culture'. Ntombisa, on the other hand, answers Jabu's question regarding the purpose of *isisu* when he says that it's to bring 'everything…out in the open so that there could be peace between the two families'. In this sense, the custom of *isisu* is useful. However, in the absence of the means to pay it, young fathers once more face the prospect of being excluded from interacting with and relating to their children. Failure to pay, or to make an arrangement to pay, means that the MOC's family makes the young man feel unwelcome, or the young man is afraid of going to see the family because then he is guilty of disrespect – and in amaXhosa culture disrespect itself carries a fine, a further financial burden on the young man or his family. This is the practice of *ukudliwa*.

The other negative aspect of damage payments is that it allows the young father's family to wield power over their son. In Lwandile's case (a young man who has never known his father and whose mother died when he was seven), his uncles and grandfather negotiated with the girl's family, paid damages and agreed to support the child on condition that Lwandile discontinued his relationship with the mother of his child:

Lwandile: I wasn't told by her. But I was told by my uncles. Her family saw her that she's pregnant… After that, they go to my family and told them. [My family] said that no, it mustn't really affect me. I mustn't be involved with the negotiations. They will negotiate without me…I want to be a lawyer. And they said…it's hard to be a lawyer…They said…we will…do what you are supposed to do for him [the child] – [sighs]. I had to agree. I had no options, because if I didn't agree, who are going to pay for the damages? So I told myself, no man, it's fine – that's a big offer for me. So, I agreed. They said it costed R5 000…You know, in our culture, *if you are a boy, you have nothing to say*. Eish, I said to myself, *if I was a man at that point – maybe they were going to come to me*…They said that we mustn't, uh, be together, because it seems like…if we can, like, be together again, we'll maybe, we will make another one. So they said no.

Lwandile's family acted on his behalf and, in their opinion, in his best interests. Lwandile was happy but conflicted at the same time. He felt he had no choice. If they had not acted as they did, he would have been forced to drop out of school. On the other hand, he seldom sees his child – no more than once a year (and then only furtively), when the mother of his child comes to visit her family in Cape Town. His relationship with her family has also deteriorated, because he is ostensibly absent from his child's life, despite the fact that his family does provide financial support for the child. Lwandile was one of the young men who volunteered to conduct social network interviews. When he reflected on the experience, he said it was extremely difficult. Because he had not been part of the negotiations, he had never confronted the family of the mother of his child. The first time he had done so was during these social network interviews. In the end, his eight social network interviews comprised his close friend, his female cousin, his grandfather, his uncle, and the cousin, uncle and two close friends of the mother of his child. He told me he was too afraid to interview either of the parents of the mother of his child, and only dared to interview her cousin and uncle after buying them 'some few beers' one Saturday afternoon, so that 'they were drunk' before he interviewed them.

In a very honest and disarming manner, male family members (and Lwandile's close friend) spoke of how culture both helped and hindered him in his quest to be a good father. Following are selected answers to seven of the eight questions from a variety of people in Lwandile's social network.

Lwandile: Do you remember how you responded when I told you that I was going to be a father? What did you say at the time? What did you think at the time?

Grandfather: I remember the day we were sitting together after I told you that now you are going to be a father, and the way you were looking like – you looked like someone who is regarding what you have done. Then I told you that you must know that we are here for you and whatever can happen to you, you have to tell us so that we can help you. You are our son. We will always stand for you.

Lwandile: What advice did you give me at the time?

Grandfather: You should be a good father when you are working. That will be your time to show that you care for your child. What I like is the fact that you know how can a child feel when he/her is growing without a father. So you need to avoid what happened to you. You need to be here for your child whenever he needs you.

Lwandile: How do you think I should have behaved differently since hearing I was going to become a father?

Grandfather: You were not supposed to act different more than going to school. You have to finish school before you do anything that can support the child, because if you try to do something now you will fail and people will say you have failed your child.

Lwandile: What kind of father do you think I have been since the time my baby was born?

Grandfather: I know that you have been a good father to the child because whenever the child needs something he gets it from us, which involves you. There is no way that you can be a bad father. We are here and will stand for you every time.

Lwandile: In what way do you think our culture has helped me to be a good father? In what way do you think our culture has stopped me from being a good father?

Grandfather: The culture forced us to stand for you at the beginning when the family had to tell you that you make their child heavy [pregnant]. So they could not talk with you because of your age. That's how the culture made you a good father. But *it also made you a bad father because of excluding you in many things that take place in the process of this.*

Close friend: I think the culture has made you to be a good father in this way on the fact that you did not have to go through the whole process because you are still young. I think if it did not happen in that way it was going to affect your studies. *And I think it stopped you from being a good father by not allowing you to go and see the child from the family of the child's mother. Now it seems like you do not care about him when he is here.*

MOC's male cousin: I am not sure of things that helped you to be a good father. And the thing that can stop you not to be a good father is your age. *The culture does not allow you to do some things because of age.*

MOC's uncle: The culture has helped you in a way that you did not have to work on your own. It forced your family to help you with the problem. *And the culture stopped you to be a good father when you were not allowed to come to the family alone, whereas your child is there.*

Lwandile: What role do you think a young father should play in the life of their children if they are not married to the mother? Should this role change over time, for example when the child is newly born, when s/he is 10, when s/he is 18 years old?

MOC's uncle: *In our culture there is no role a young father can play.* It's only his family that can do anything for the sake of the child. It's only the family that can do anything.

Grandfather: *According to me a young father is supposed to do nothing but being helped by his family. Unless he was working;* then he can play a big role there by supporting the child all the way.

Lwandile: Why do you think young men often lose contact with their children over the years?

MOC's uncle: *The culture can be one of the causes of losing the contact because if you are a young father sometimes you have no say.* So there is someone to decide for you.

Grandfather: It's because of not listening to their family so the family cannot help them. If they are not working with them and if the boy has never gave the family respect, they won't do anything for him.

An alternative to excluding fathers from interacting with the MOC's family

In contrast to Lwandile's social network interviews (and those of Onathi and Vuyo), Siya's social network interviews included the MOC's mother and father (in addition to his own father, two close friends, his grandmother, the mother of his child and her sister). Responses from both parents of the mother of his child are reproduced below, although the interviews were conducted separately.

Siya: Do you remember how you responded when I told you that I was going to be a father? What did you say at the time? What did you think at the time?

MOC's mother: Yes, I remember the time I was responding to you, and I told you that you thought being a father is a simple thing. I thought you were joking.

MOC's father: Yes, I asked you that how many times did I tell you that you must be wise in your relationship and play safe. I told you this because I knew the risks you were to face at this stage of your life. At the time *I was thinking of my financial problem to solve this trouble.*

Siya: What advice did you give me at the time?

MOC's mother: I told you to go and seek for a job to the factory and prepare for being a father, as you would like your father to do. At that time, I was taking it for granted that you will be a father.

MOC's father: I told you some ways of facing and overcoming such problems in your life. I've made some examples that are similar to what you did, and gave you a way of approaching it.

Siya: How do you think I should have behaved differently since hearing I was going to become a father?

MOC's mother: I thought you were going to change your behaviour and you will be stressed becoming a father. I thought you were going to start working on your dignity and respect.

MOC's father: I thought that you should have a way of doing things, as you saw the big mistake you did. *I thought you were going to change your social behaviour and try being more grown up.*

Siya: What kind of father do you think I have been since the time my baby was born?

MOC's mother: You were the father that was very shy, and you were taking care of your baby. You enjoyed your child's company very much.

MOC's father: A father that is not hiding the fact that he is a father in front of me, and *you do meet with your family regularly to provide love and care.*

Siya: In what way do you think our culture has helped me to be a good father? In what way do you think our culture has stopped me from being a good father?

MOC's mother: Our culture helped you to be a good father in the way that you became a dignified and respected father, as *our culture is against the fact that young fathers disappear in the mist.*

MOC's father: Our culture has helped you to accept that you are a father, and you should be a father that satisfies his family and meet the challenges of being a father.

Siya: What role do you think a young father should play in the life of their children if they are not married to the mother? Should this role change over time, for example when the child is newly born, when s/he is 10, when s/he is 18 years old?

MOC's mother: *During the time a father is young he should not play any role.* Their parents, the father's parents, should play a vital role to represent the young man until the father is working and take responsibility from then.

MOC's father: I think you should leave the things to your parents while you at school, but after you done start to take the responsibility of being a father.

Siya: Why do you think young men often lose contact with their children over the years?

MOC's mother: Sometimes the young mothers are the reason for the fathers to lose contact, as they do not value the effort the father is making towards the child's life.

MOC's father: I think young men start to develop some minds after they stay away from their children, because of the minds that they had before.

Siya: What advice do you have for me about being a young father in the future?

MOC's mother: Young fathers should be contented fathers and accept what has happened, and go forward, and do things with extra care, avoiding doing the same mistake.

MOC's father: When you start to work, the first thing that should be in your mind is that you are a father. *Take responsibility of being a father.* Have some plans of your young child for the future.

Their responses are short and candid yet indicate the existence of a relationship between the young father and the MOC's parents – a phenomenon seldom encountered between the other young fathers and the MOC's parents (with some exceptions). When Siya was asked why this might be the case, he had a ready answer:

Siya: It was very difficult for her to tell me that I got her pregnant because of my reputation as far as girls was concerned…it wasn't easy in terms of telling her family. [But] I told her no, no wait, I'll tell them myself. *I told them myself and then the negotiations can carry on from there but I want to tell them myself…*Her father was like shouting – all that kind of stuff but he knew that we had something going on between me and her and then…I made the father understand…*I was very like polite* and then I was…telling him that what happened is a mistake but I don't want to say that my child is a mistake because at the end of the day he is my child. So he said that I was making a child drop out of school, and I said no, if you are saying that I'm also prepared to drop out of school for her, so that me and her can both raise the baby. So that is what happened, we both dropped out for a year at school.

So it was that part of a story that I was forced to negotiate with old people of which it was something a 14-year-old by himself can't just do…

Like Vee's parents were mostly negotiating with my uncle…We were forced to pay a certain amount of which it was R2 500. I was just there when I was going to tell them that Vee is pregnant. You see, what I believed in was my uncle and my brothers and sisters were not there when me and Vee were making the baby. *So the people who have to be responsible for it is the people who were actually making babies. So we both went [to tell her parents but]…I left it to my uncle to do the negotiation.* What I was to do was to deliver the news.

In many respects Siya's behaviour broke with traditional amaXhosa custom. At the same time, he was aware of the custom and let his uncles take over the negotiations and did not participate further. But his insistence on facing the mother of his child's father, admitting his mistake and outlining his plan to deal with it earned him her father's respect, and ultimately contributed to Siya giving up his other partners (named for days of the week) and committing himself to an exclusive relationship with Vee. At the time of the study, Siya was only 17 years old. Yet he successfully negotiated through a turbulent period in the life of a young man who discovers he is to be a father at the age of 14. He dropped out of school and took on a menial job in a hardware store for a year. He then returned to school and worked part-time at a funeral parlour in order to contribute to his child's support. He remade contact with his biological father, who was absent for most of his life, and is rebuilding that relationship. He regularly sees his child and the mother of his child, with whom he remains in a relationship, despite the fact that they are temporarily geographically separated to enable him to go to a good Western Cape school. He has become a man in the amaXhosa tradition, earlier than usual so that his son can call him father rather than by his first name (which is the custom if you are still *inkwenkwe* – a boy). He has considered plans for the future, which include a good career and building a future for his son and his son's mother.

Conclusion

The literature has much to say about the young father's relationship with the mother of his child (Kalil et al. 2005; Quinton et al. 2002) and with the family of the mother of his child, noting how significant they are in facilitating or impeding a young father's involvement with his child (Devault et al. 2008; Kiselica 1995; Miller 1997). Both serve as 'gatekeepers' (Herzog et al. 2007) to the child. In fact, positive relationships with the mother of the child, although not necessarily as a couple, predict a greater likelihood of sustained involvement, according to Kalil et al. (2005). Kalil et al. also find that where relationships between the young father and the MOC are strained or antagonistic, or where the MOC is stressed or depressed, young fathers are less likely to be involved.

Furthermore, the mother of the MOC has been shown to impact on a young father's relationship with his child in two ways. Where her support for her daughter and grandchild is *too* strong, young fathers show low and decreasing involvement over time. However, when the MOC's mother has a good relationship with the young father (Krishnakumar & Black 2003) and is *moderately supportive* (Kalil et al. 2005), young fathers are found to be highly involved. In addition, when the MOC has a good relationship with the young father's mother, involvement is further improved (Kalil et al. 2005).

The literature, however, has less to say on the role that young fathers' own mothers play in helping or hindering his involvement with his child. In this study, young men attribute an enormous role to their mothers in enabling them to be good fathers. Studies by Bucklin (1999), Fagan et al. (2007) and Anderson (1993b) corroborate this important finding. Specifically, in a small study of 34 American young fathers, Bucklin found a statistically significant relationship between the teen fathers' attachments to their own mothers and higher levels of physical and emotional caretaking of their children. Fagan et al. found that their mothers' support buffered young fathers' reported stress. Anderson found that the mother's acceptance of her son's paternity and her feelings towards the MOC helped the young man to accept his paternity and adopt a parenting role. Clearly, young men's mothers play an important role. However, their influence can also be too overbearing when they accept too much responsibility for the young father's child, and effectively discourage him from parental involvement.

It is not surprising that parents, especially mothers, play such a crucial role in the lives of their sons and daughters who become parents at a young age. In many senses their children are in fact still that – 'children having children',[23] and they remain under the guardianship of their parents in terms of both the customary and formal legal systems, which reveals the inevitable dilemmas and controversies in parents' involvement in the rearing of their children's children without taking over.

Finally, regarding the impact of culture on young fathers' involvement with their children, the literature is still in its infancy. A few authors, such as Chikovore et al. (2003), are beginning to speak of the role of *ilobolo* and damage payments on young men's ability to form households, with the subsequent impact on the security and rights of children (Himonga 2001) who have no inheritance rights and less chance of being able to obtain support legally.[24] However, traditional patriarchal models that negotiate childcare arrangements on behalf of a young man, leaving him with 'nothing to say', and the overwhelming financial demands felt by young fathers from traditional cultures (or perhaps just impoverished communities, in the case of the young 'coloured' fathers in this study) frequently result in young fathers deserting, denying paternity or becoming disinterested in their child (Ramphele 2002; Rhein et al. 1997). The complicity of traditional cultural practices as a hindering factor to ongoing father involvement needs to be considered further. At the same time, its many positive features and protective practices – such as initiation schools and *mephato* peer groups (Lesejane 2006) and the practice of collective parenting through extended families (Mkhize 2006) – need to be celebrated.

23 A child is a person under 18 years, unless emancipated by marriage – an act which requires permission from the minister of home affairs.
24 The Children's Act (No. 38 of 2005) and the Children's Amendment Act (No. 41 of 2007) change this substantially. However, the perception surrounding legal marriage being stronger than customary marriage or no marriage at all remains, and frequently provides an artificial barrier to those seeking financial support for their children.

CHAPTER 6

'Spare wheels' and 'meat to meat': The meaning of sexual health for impoverished young men

When we met with a group of young fathers at the end of the study to debrief and consult with them regarding the findings of this study, the mood in the room changed markedly when they read and responded to this chapter. Up until then the discussion had been lively and animated. When they digested the fact that this chapter's discussion of their failure to use condoms and their proclivity towards MCPs portrayed them as irresponsible young men, they grew silent and lowered their heads. In response to their disappointment, they were asked whether this chapter should therefore be excluded. The reply was a unanimous 'no'. Instead, they argued that policy-makers and people who worked with youth needed to understand the reality of their lives, where their choice to be *pleyas* (sexually active with a number of girls) was one they made in contrast to choosing to be *gangstas* (criminals).[25] Onathi commented: 'Being poor, I don't have possessions but I can possess lots of women.'

This chapter therefore begins by discussing condoms as a currency of trust among young men and the ways in which multiple (and frequently) concurrent sexual partnerships interact to put these young fathers at risk of HIV infection and (further) future mistimed fathering. It also interrogates the dearth of services and notes how sex education (from school and family) has failed these young men.

Young fathers' use of condoms and knowledge of contraception

Failure to use condoms was probably the chief reason why young men found themselves as fathers 'before time'. In Chapter 3 these young fathers described candidly why they failed to use condoms. At the top of the list was the issue of pleasure – 'skin to skin' or 'meat to meat' provided the most sexual pleasure, followed closely by how alcohol and 'the heat of the moment' made them 'careless'. But another reason also featured strongly, that of trust. Young men were reluctant to use condoms with a steady partner (or even steady partners) out of fear that she would think that he was sleeping with other girls (frequently the case), a fact that would jeopardise her fidelity to him. A number of young fathers also spoke about their ignorance of condoms when they first started having sex at age 13, 14 or 15, and how this ignorance was compounded if one had newly arrived from a rural area (*ibari*) and was trying to fit in with the 'no condom' culture of township life. In response to our attempt to probe deeper, young men valiantly tried to articulate their responses.

---

25 Although failure to use condoms was a shared characteristic between both 'black' and 'coloured' young fathers, it was young 'black' men who seemed to have more multiple concurrent partners. Also, young 'coloured' men spoke of their relationships with greater intensity and the possibilities of marriage far more frequently than did the young 'black' men in this study.

The power of desire and pressure to be condom-free

In speaking of the power of desire, Onathi first described how sex is better without a condom before going on to say that when asked by his grandmother about his condom use, he lied, saying it was a one-time mistake instead of telling her his true feelings about condoms, i.e. 'to hell with the condom':

Onathi: Okay, maybe honestly, like – not using a condom, mmm, there's a big difference when using condom than not using condom. There's a big difference. Without a condom, but – yah, it's better but it's – I mean, when you're not using a condom there's a lot of damages can happen. HIV/AIDS, pregnancy. But, that's why other people don't use condom all the time – because it feels better, yah.

     [My grandmother] asked didn't I use a condom, all this stuff. Why didn't I use a condom? *Eish* – she understands I'm a man now. And I'm old. I know about sex…I told her, 'It was a mistake, I'm sorry.' All that stuff. 'It won't happen again. It was a one-time thing.' Like I never said 'to hell with the condom'.

Luxolo and Tapelo then spoke about how 'girls agree' to not using condoms after 'some romance' (especially 'if she is innocent') and that neither partner thinks about pregnancy at the time:

Luxolo: What I can say now [pause]. After you have a girlfriend, taken her on a date, kissed her, and make some romance – you not going to use a condom any more, you see. And the girl agrees – she says, 'I love him'. And I'm saying you can't eat a sweet that has got a paper – so you can't use a condom with this girl! I love her. I don't think I can use a condom any more. If she was taking care of herself, *if she is innocent* – I can't use a condom.

Tapelo: Sometimes when you talk with a girl, I ask her if we must use a condom, then she said no. And I asked her why, she said the condom is not good for her. And other guys they say it's not good with the condom…They don't think about pregnancy at that time. Because you see it's still nice at that time when she is not pregnant, and by the time she is pregnant she starts to think.

Condoms as the currency of trust

Young men expanded on how condom use is a currency of trust when they spoke of using condoms with some partners but not others. Onathi explained that with his other girlfriends he used condoms but when he settled into an exclusive relationship he stopped using them. Luthando was more explicit and told of how his girlfriend took it as an indication of fidelity that they didn't use condoms, while Lwethu spoke of getting into the habit of not using condoms with one partner and then carrying on the practice with others:

Onathi: Because she was my only girlfriend, and, like – I'm gonna say, like, I trusted her…I knew she wasn't sleeping with other guys…I trusted her…So I didn't – and I knew myself, that I'm not sleeping [with] other women, so I did it. That's what happened…so, I didn't use it with her, but the others…not without condom.

Interviewer: How come you used a condom with the other girlfriends before Tee?

Onathi: I didn't trust them that much as – I don't think I'm the – I'm the only guy there, so, yah. I didn't take chances like that. I didn't take chances like that.

Luthando: My girlfriend doesn't want me to use condom. It's like I don't trust her, when I use condom.

Lwethu: When we were together, I trusted her, she trusted me, so we didn't use condoms. We only used condoms when we were having sex with other people around. So, we decided to not use condoms. Every time I was with her, I was so used to the thing that no condom, no condom, no condom, yah. *Then it became – hard to – to use a condom with others.*

Ignorance about contraception and condoms

Seventeen-year-old Lwandile (15 when he had a child) spoke of how he was ignorant about sex and condoms when he arrived in Cape Town from the rural areas of the Eastern Cape. Exacerbating his ignorance was the pressure he felt to fit in, to act like a *gangsta* – and among the latter young men 'using condoms was not popular that much':

Lwandile: My friends were not using it [laughs]. So, uh, I said to myself, 'No man, I mustn't use it because, uh, I don't have, uh, enough information about it.' Even if – I don't have even enough information [about] how to put it – in my [clears throat noisily] – in my, on my thing. So, I said to myself, 'No man, it's hard to start something that you, like, don't know how it works' [laughs]…At that point – like I was training for living in Cape Town – you know *mos* when, uh, you are trying to be like a *gangsta*? I was like training – *I have to be like them. So no condom.*

Lonwabo and Tapelo also spoke of their ignorance and fear about using condoms. For Lonwabo, at '13 or 14' he did not have 'the information about how condoms, all that stuff, you see', while Tapelo simply 'didn't think about condoms that time and I was scared to go to the clinic and take the condoms. I think they would have shouted at me.' Young fathers' ignorance extended also to general knowledge about contraceptives, illustrated perhaps most starkly by Luthando and Jabu:

Luthando: She said to me…she took an injection for five years, five years injection. So that she will not have a baby [laughs] for five years.

Jabu: I think it's like that, because I didn't care about the condom. I thought it was for old people.

In Luthando's and Xolile's views, young women frequently refused contraception, not only because of trust issues but also because of their fears of what it would do to their bodies:

Xolile: The girls don't want to use injection because they believe it mess with their body – so that when they got married and they want a baby, they couldn't even get the baby there.

Luthando: The girls they don't want to get injection. I ask her, 'What if we have a kid?' 'No, no, no, don't tell me about that. I don't want do that cos it will make me fatter.'

Condom use escalates after the baby arrives

No matter what young men's views were about why they did not use condoms or encourage their partners to use contraception, most were in agreement that after their child was born, condom use escalated so that they did not repeat their 'mistake':

Saki: I know that I've been using condom ever since then [baby].

Vuyo: Now, I use condom, because I was learn a lesson…I'm not ready to get, eh, another baby.

Fadiel: I use condoms now because I had a shock, yes.

These young fathers spoke easily about the need for condoms and contraception, yet said very little about the MCPs in which many were involved.

The allure of emotional connection through multiple partners

The practice of MCPs is perhaps one of the biggest drivers of HIV in sub-Saharan Africa (Halperin & Epstein 2007). Young fathers (and young men in general) put themselves at enormous risk through practising unprotected sex with multiple partners, each of whom, in turn, may be part of a potentially infected network of partners. For this reason, the existence among these young fathers of numerous multiple partner relationships is a significant and important discussion. Of the young 'black' men participating in this study, three-quarters reported involvement in MCPs (compared to one-third of the young 'coloured' participants).

Lwethu, the young man from Langa doing 'loxion management', i.e. who is unemployed after passing matric, became a father in 2007. His explanation of why he had multiple partners was perhaps the most comprehensive. He began by speaking of the number of sexual partners he had and how he managed them:

Interviewer: How many other girlfriends do you have?

Lwethu: At school I had three – then two outside of school. So, it was five.

Interviewer: Five. And were you having sex with all five, or only some of them?

Lwethu: All.

Interviewer: And what's the reason for having so many?

Lwethu: The reason to have five girlfriends is so that if somebody drops you – you have a spare wheel…Let me explain for you. Eh, before I was a *pleya* – before everything, before I had many girlfriends, I was a one-woman man, you see? So, what happens is – is that we always fall in love with the wrong girl, you see? Tell yourself, 'I'm in love, I'm in love, I don't want another girl, I don't want another girl.' Then you get heartbroken. So, you get heartbroken for months and months. It's hard to get another girlfriend. Then, once you get another girlfriend, you tell yourself, *I must not have one, I must have a spare wheel, because if I get heartbroken here, at least I have something on the side, you see?* That's why we become *pleyas*.

Interviewer: So how do you manage having so many girls? Don't they find out about each other?

Lwethu: When one finds me with another, I just act relaxed so that they cannot see that, oh, this is your girlfriend. Just act relaxed and, 'Hi, how are you?' then I'll pass. She's gonna ask me later on, 'Who was that?' 'She was my cousin,' I'll tell her – so [laughs].

Interviewer: So you need a spare wheel, uh? Are *pleyas* boys or men? *Inkwenkwe* or *indoda*?

Lwethu: *When you go to the bush – it makes you worse* [laughs]. Makes you worse. I don't know why. Because, when you're wearing all that – I was wearing a blanket. I'm kind of like seSotho, you see. And the girls are like, hoohoo, crazy about you, crazy, crazy, crazy – because I'm a man now. *Especially the first months when you're* ikrwala [new initiate]. You end up having like 20 or 30 girls – some others when they call me, you forget, 'Who are you?' [you ask].

Interviewer: But why, Lwethu, why do you need so many girls? Aren't you tired of managing all these relationships?

Lwethu: Um, I'm not tired yet. Cos there – there are still people, uh, I'm looking at and seeing, ag, I like that girl, you see? I still – I still need more. I don't know why.

Interviewer: What do you need more of? Love or sex? Which one is it?

Lwethu: *Attention – I'm not that into sex.* [Although] with some girls I wouldn't say that we have a relationship – it's just strictly sex – [but] I'm not – *I'm not that into it. I just love the attention*…Originally I'm not a *pleya*, and I know that I can reduce –

Interviewer: You can stop being a *pleya*?

Lwethu: I can stop. Immediately, I get the girl, the right – 'Miss Right'. I can immediately stop…But I don't know, uh. It's something with – *it's always with – our people, I don't know what's – what's wrong with my people.*

Lwethu makes three very interesting points. He speaks of the need to have a 'spare wheel' – a sentiment shared by many other young 'black' men. Like young men's fear of their parents, this seems to be a strange response to the possibility of disappointment in intimate relationships. Why should young men be so afraid of the end of a relationship that they need a 'spare'? As with fear of parents (over becoming a young father), does this, too, have to do with loss of face, or shame, not in relation to their parents and transgressing a strong cultural bond, but with friends – transgressing an *ikasi* youth cultural custom? In addition, Lwethu implies that having multiple partners is not simply about an insatiable sexual appetite. Many young men speak of attractions other than sex – like attention and status, and being 'top dog' rather than *isishumani* (shoemaker, a colloquial term that can also mean someone who can only manage one girlfriend) among their peers (Swartz 2007).

It was not unusual to hear young fathers speak about truly loving one of their partners, but that 'yes, there are others; but I love her'. Xolile began by saying that the mother of his child was the one he truly loved but then continued:

Xolile: I was – okay – I was with – [whistles] – [long pause] four, yah.

Interviewer: So, you've been having sex with four other girlfriends while you've been together with the mother of your child?

Xolile: Yah, yah.

Interviewer: And does your girlfriend know?

Xolile: No.

Interviewer: And what would she say if she knew?

Xolile: She would be angry with me. So, that's why I decided to, no, to be cut with them, to concentrate to her...but I still have them.

Interviewer: And condoms?

Xolile: No condoms – I'm using no condoms with [any of] them.

Xolile's behaviour places him at risk of HIV, of further pregnancies with multiple young women, and also of losing contact with his child should the mother of his child – the one on whom he is trying 'to concentrate' – find out about his other partners. Often when the mother's family finds out about the young father's other concurrent sexual partnerships, in support of their daughter they 'refuse to open the door when I knock, even though I can hear people inside' (as told by Yusuf).

So, while young men regularly have MCPs, and some accuse their partners of having other partners as well, only two spoke of how MCPs can damage relationships. Most were not strongly in favour of limiting partnerships, either for health reasons or to remain on good terms with the mother of their child. Siya, the young man who called his sexual partners by the days of the week, said:

Siya: I am now kinda embarrassed for that I did such things to them because, um, as I told you I am mostly involved in the NGOs. So I got to hear what actually the females feel about this kind of behaviour, and it broke my heart because I was one of those guys who does those things.

Dumisani took his analysis a step further by saying that MCPs damage your relationship with your child because having multiple partners costs money, and the money you spend on them could have been spent on your child:

Dumisani: It's only one thing – it was women who were disturbing me...I had other girlfriends besides the mother of my child and they wanted me to focus on them most of the time. For instance, here in Durban – girls in Durban require money a lot. So if you have to deal with them – even if you can have money – you will spend it with her and at the end of the day you are unable to support your child, whereas you are wasting money with other people who will not help you in any way.

During the debriefing and consultation workshop, young men added that 'having multiple partners' made you enemies – from 'the girls who find out about each other' to the 'guys who are jealous that you have so many girls and they have none'. In general, young men did not speak of multiple partners with bravado, but merely as a fact of *ikasi* life. But neither did they speak of MCPs as something to be avoided. In fact, only a few young fathers described a good father as someone 'who is not seen with many women when he has a child with another woman – he must have one straight partner' (S'bu). So it's not the fact of multiple partners per se that young men regard as a problem, but rather, having multiple partners when one has a child.

In later interviews, when young fathers were asked about what they would do to help their son or daughter avoid early parenthood, not one mentioned either abstinence or monogamous relationships. Rather, they felt strongly about teaching their child – son or daughter – to use contraception. Similarly, their role models – adult men in the community – were frequently involved in MCPs, and many young fathers were in families where their own fathers were 'faithless'. In a social network interview with a teacher, Onathi asked, 'Why do you think young men often lose contact with their children over the years?' to which his teacher, rather candidly, replied:

Onathi's teacher: I think it's because of girlfriends and because we see, like me too, like when I grew up I've been seeing these girls, although I'm married to my wife. I just watch this girl, and then I will want to just – to have her. Just – just a sense of want, not a need. Yah.

In contrast to the young 'black' fathers in this study, fewer young 'coloured' fathers were involved in MCPs. In fact, only Fadiel had two 'girlfriends' at the same time, although with disastrous consequences – he got both of them pregnant at the same time, and his two children were born within a week of each other when he was 17. He explained what happened:

Fadiel: She knew I did have another girlfriend but she didn't catch me yet. See?…There's nothing she can do because I'm the child's father but you could see inside – you could see that she was very hurt…

I loved both of them…my first girlfriend I – we were, we had [an argument or] something, so we left each other. So I took the second girlfriend. Then we were an item and then the first girlfriend came, then she came to me again and said she wanted to get together again. I felt something for her. Because we were, we were together for a long time since primary school, we were always checking each other out. Then it happened that the second girl-friend didn't want to leave either and I couldn't chase her away. See?

Besides the health risks arising out of MCPs, a further analysis of the data also shows how multiple part-nerships, especially at the time of conception of the child, seem to be associated with young fathers not being in a relationship with the mother of their child in the one to four years following the birth of their child. Table 6.1 records the trajectory of the relationship for each of the young men in the study and allows for a number of interesting observations to be made. Of the young men in the sam-ple, fewer were involved in exclusive committed relationships (8 out of 27, or 30 per cent) than were involved in either non-exclusive (12 out of 27, or 44 per cent) or casual relationships (7 out of 27, or 26 per cent). Young men whose fathering resulted from causal encounters were just as likely to envisage a future together with the mother of their child as were those who were involved in non-exclusive but committed relationships – although in both cases this applied to about half of the young men in the study in either category.[26] Of those young men involved in committed and exclusive relationships, all but one (11 out of 12) envisaged a future with the mother of their child.

---

26   Six out of 12 (50 per cent) of the young men involved in a non-exclusive relationship which they described as being 'together' with the mother of their child said they envisaged a future with the mother of their child, while 3 out of 7 (43 per cent) who described their relationships as 'casual' envisaged a future with the mother of their child.

TABLE 6.1   *The relationship trajectory between young fathers and the mother of their child*

Name	At conception	At birth and afterwards	Current	Future
Casual encounters				
Jabu	Not together	Not together	Not together	Not together
Lonwabo	Not together	Not together	Not together	Not together
Lwethu	Not together	Not together	Not together	Not together
Nhlanhla	Not together	Together	Together	Together
Ntombisa	Not together	Not together	Not together	Together
Sifiso	Not together	Not together	Not together	Not together
Siya	Not together	Together	Together	Together
Non-exclusive relationships				
Bongani	Together	Not together	Not together	Not together
Dumisani	Not together	Not together	Not together	Not together
Fadiel*	Together	Together	Together/Not together	Together/Not together
Lungile	Together	Together	Together	Together
Luxolo	Together	Together	Not together	Not together
Lwandile	Not together	Not together	Not together	Together
Sakhile	Together	Together	Together	Together
Tapelo	Not together	Together	Not together	Not together
Vuyo	Together	Not together	Not together	Not together
Xolile	Together	Together	Together	Together
Yusuf	Together	Not together	Not together	Not together
Exclusive relationships				
Andile	Together	Together	Together	Together
Ibrahiem	Together	Together	Together	Together
Luthando	Together	Together	Together	Together
Marlin	Together	Together	Together	Together
Onathi	Together	Together	Together	Together
S'bu	Together	Together	Together	Together
Sabier	Together	Together	Together	Together
Saki	Together	Together	Not together	Not together
Zaid	Together	Together	Together	Together

*Fadiel has two children, each from a different woman.

Young men who fathered a child while being in a non-exclusive relationship seldom converted to an exclusive relationship once the child was born. Of the eight young men who classified themselves in this category, at the time of the study only one was involved in an exclusive relationship with the mother of his child, one was involved in a non-exclusive relationship with the mother of his child, and Fadiel, the young man who fathered two children with two young women simultaneously, was in a committed, exclusive relationship with one of them. This was similar in the case of young men who had fathered a child during a casual encounter – only two had converted the relationship into an exclusive, committed relationship. In contrast, young men who were involved in committed relationships when they fathered their child were three to four times more likely to be in an exclusive relationship with the mother of their child (9 out of 12, or 75 per cent, were in exclusive, committed relationships at the time of the study).

Of the 27 cases described in this study, the families of seven young fathers were physically involved in the day-to-day caring for the child (apart from only providing financial support). In five cases, this occurred when the young father and the mother of his child were currently together as a couple, although in two cases (Jabu and Saki) they were not together – Saki's parents took care of his child and Jabu's sister took care of his child. In both these cases, the mother of the child did not want to be involved in raising the child. In neither case do the young father and the mother of his child have plans to be together in the future.

The dearth of services and failure of sex education

Earlier in this chapter, Tapelo described his fear of going to clinics, reflecting many other young fathers' reluctance to use the clinics in their area. Xolile knew of a 'clinic for men's problems' at his local taxi rank in Kuwait, Khayelitsha, but never went there, while for Lwandile and Lwethu, clinics were best avoided:

Lwandile: The clinics are very, very far from us as the youth. We don't want to go there, even myself.

Lwethu: I went with her when she was going for shots – when Nee [his daughter] was going for – I think it was six months – for her shots. I went. I never went back there. It's been a while now.

Interviewer: When you did go, did they speak to you, the nurses or sisters?

Lwethu: No, they just do what you came here to do. No discussion, no nothing.

Young men seldom made use of other available services. Yusuf told of 'hearing about things like that [life skills courses being run at the] multipurpose centre [in Bonteheuwel]' but said that 'I haven't gone'. Only Saki got a social worker involved when it came to deciding about custody. None had gone to court, although Yusuf was thinking about going to force the mother of his child to allow him to see the child. It seems that for most of these young men, 'black' and 'coloured' alike, childcare arrangements are settled through family negotiation, with young men playing a lesser or greater role in the discussion depending on the involvement and support of their parents and their status as a boy or a man (especially in isiXhosa culture).

Also, for most of the young men, participating in this study was the first time they had spoken to someone (outside of their immediate family) about their experiences and struggles as a young father. Most had not heard of programmes for young fathers, although a number of them cited the 'Positive

Sexuality' course run by loveLife and those who had attended it found it helpful. In addition, just as many of these young fathers had turned to using condoms after the arrival of their child, a number of them had gone to find out about general life skills workshops being run by Planned Parenthood, the University of Cape Town (at a library in Khayelitsha) and loveLife (especially those who were still in school). Only Siya mentioned *a specific programme for young fathers* being run at a Baptist church in Langa by someone who had been a young parent, in addition to his involvement at loveLife:

Siya: I'm a person who likes attending formal things. I used to attend community upliftments where they talk about single parents and all that kind of stuff. So, I was quite involved then in church societies where they give advice as to young people who have children…for example, I was once a Groundbreaker [peer educator] at loveLife and then we used to talk about teenage pregnancy and all that kind of stuff…

          There were workshops at church because I was, er, going to church back in the days. So, um, they knew that we were a couple of young mens and ladies that we had children and then there [were] classes for us teaching us how to – *to be there for our children*, how to make sure that we were there, in fact in all of their lives…It was very helpful, it was very helpful! Because we were *getting an advice from a person who was became a young parent back in his life!*

loveLife's programmes seemed to be well known among these young fathers:

Lwandile: I've been involved in loveLife only from a few months ago. When you are there you learn more!…They make sure that when you are [leave] you won't have that ignorance…So, if loveLife was there for me on that time, I think, I personally think this was not going to happen!

Interviewer: And why wasn't loveLife there for you? I mean, you were here in Langa and loveLife was in Langa?

Lwandile: [Laughs] Firstly, there are some who doesn't know that you are having loveLife around. And, uh, I was one of them…But there's some people who knows that there is loveLife but they are ignoring it cos they think that when you are in loveLife you have to test for AIDS, you have to prevent, you have to do things that they don't want to do! Because there is some people who have that knowledge but they ignore the fact that knowledge is power.

S'bu: Programmes like loveLife are only found in clinics. You don't see or hear about them in the flats where people live, or here in shacks. You only find them in clinics, but if they were closer to the people I think there wouldn't be [so] much problems.

Lwethu: At loveLife there are nurses you can go and talk to, and people you can go and talk to there. I never – I never did. I never thought of going.

So while young men knew of *general* sexual health programmes available to them, few made use of their services. A number reflected Nhlanhla's view that they 'didn't think there are any programmes [for young fathers] because once you are a father you are a man'.

HIV testing

When it came to knowing their status and being tested for HIV, the majority of young men (fewer from KwaZulu-Natal than from the Western Cape) had been tested and did know their status. Among the Cape Town-based isiXhosa young fathers who were *indoda*, HIV testing had been a mandatory part of their *ulwaluko* rite of passage. Others had gone for a test when they had decided to 'get serious with one partner'. Others, when asked about their HIV status, had inferred they were negative because the mother of their child was negative and they used condoms with other partners. Overall, these young men seemed to be well informed about the necessity of voluntary counselling and testing, and where they could get tested:

Nhlanhla: When my girlfriend was pregnant with this child, we went to the hospital and they tested us. There is free testing. And it's written all over about the importance of knowing your status.

Onathi: When Tee told me she was pregnant. Then I – first thing I ask, 'Did you go check for the HIV test?' She said, 'Not yet, but when you're pregnant you must check HIV, yah.' So it was worrying me. But when she come back and told me that no, she's negative, then I told myself, 'I'm also negative'. If she doesn't have it, then I don't have to go there and test myself, no. I didn't go and test, no.

Luxolo: I know. I'm negative. I [test] at day hospital. Day hospital. Because I'm risking.

Bongani: I've never tested [but my child] I heard that he's fine and then I thought that it means I'm also fine.

Siya: I've been to a test and it was late last year before me going to the initiation school. Of which I was negative.

Tapelo: And even this year I did it. Because you see I've got another girlfriend now and she said she wants to trust me and I also said I want to trust her. So we go together.

Sex education

When it came to sex education, young men were clear about two issues: firstly, their parents, especially their fathers, did not talk frankly with them about 'sex and making children', and secondly, school sex education did not meet their needs:

Fadiel: My father never didn't speak to me about those kinds of things. Nobody actually…He never sat down with me to talk like – but he – he didn't talk about sex and making children and so on…But I will do that for my children.

Zaid: Most parents, they don't speak to the children about it. They don't speak to the children about sex or anything. They rather [say] if there's maybe a 16 restriction on the TV and then, 'Put the TV off. It's sex on TV again.' Like that but they won't come face to face with their children now, like talk. I like – in Life Orientation [school subject], I enjoyed that stuff. Cos there, they're open and they speak about it and there's pictures and stuff like that, man, which our parents don't do to us so…If your mother tells you something, it almost go, it's like, it's like it goes here in and it comes there out [pointing to one ear and then another in turn]. Now, your friend tells you something like out of the blue. Then you're also checking,

'Why is this man talking this way?' And he's not [normally serious] like this. So it's almost like, you will listen to your friend – than listen to your mommy.

Only Saki spoke of having parents who could speak openly about relationships:

Saki: I could talk at home. If I've got a problem with my girlfriend, we talk. Just like that. Like we grew – it's more like we grew up in a white family.

When asked why sex education was not helpful, a number of young people replied that it was because they were too 'playful' when they were young and rarely listened:

Jabu: Cos back – back then I was so playful [pause]. Yah. I didn't totally take notice of things, of serious things. Because like, um, I took things as a joke.

Onathi: Whenever the teachers are maybe teaching us about sex…we said, 'No, no, man, don't talk nonsense, man. Don't talk nonsense.' We don't listen. Yah, we don't listen [laughs]. I really don't know what would make me listen. Because my parents tried, and I – and I didn't listen. So, I won't say it's them, because I didn't listen to them. So I – I don't know what will make me listen. But now I listen. There's no way in hell I'll do it again [get someone pregnant].

Tapelo: You see, at the time you are in school you don't listen. You tell yourself that he talking nonsense.

Others were more critical, saying that teachers set bad examples by sleeping with students and in so doing relinquished their right to teach young people about sex:

Xolile: Teachers, they're gonna start with themselves, because teachers at school, I know – we know the teachers. They are sleeping with students. We see them. So, how can they tell us 'I told you no' when we see it's them. How can you just told us to just quit sex? Because we see now you're sleeping with the girls at school, in classes, after school.

Others, such as Nhlanhla, Lwethu, Zaid and Vuyo, provided some constructive suggestions for improvement, including speaking about 'AIDS-fatigue' (weariness of talking about HIV/AIDS) among students; the need to speak about the relationship between alcohol and sex; that the approach should be peer to peer; and that Life Orientation should include more 'activities outside':

Nhlanhla: Yah, I don't think it's [sex education at school] enough. Because you know, at schools they only talk about [pause] – they say you'll get AIDS. Everybody knows about AIDS.

Lwethu: Young people should talk to young people. Cos if you're an old person come to talk to a young person, just ignores you, gets in this way, and gets out that way [point to ears]…You have to take views, views, views, views. And discuss what should be done…Don't just say, 'This is wrong'…Don't just lecture. Listen to their views. And ask what would make them to stop and everything. Just discuss, and maybe the conclusion will come.

Zaid: But Life Orientation…It's activities, face-to-face activities, or we're outside on the field, we're doing activities outside. So it's fun. I think that they must actually make more time for Life Orientation.

Vuyo: They must talk also about drinking at school. Not just sex.

Sex education in modern times

When asked how they would treat their own child if they came to them at the age of 15 to say they had made someone pregnant or had become pregnant, young men were almost unanimous in declaring their support for the child. Only Sakhile said that he would throw his child out of the house and demand that he go and work to support his child. But young men were also clear that it was preferable if it never got to that:

Lwethu: I've never prepared myself to – to have an experience like that. No, obviously I'm gonna – I'm gonna give her [his child] advice while she's growing up to make the right choices and everything. So, I hope it won't get to that.

Young fathers made it clear that, unlike their parents, they intended to speak to their children about sex from a young age:

Xolile: As a parent, most of the time they're scared to talk about sex to their daughter and sons.

Interviewer: And you?

Xolile: No, me, I don't even talk with my parents with that.

Interviewer: Yah, but for your son?

Xolile: I can do that, because – because we know our parents. They're still old – they are for traditions. So now, right now, we are born to another traditions now. So we know what is happening outside now. Because even at our schools, they teach sex education because HIV and AIDS and also STDs [sexually transmitted diseases]. So I must tell him, 'No, son, I don't want to control your life, but be careful because there's these – these HIV and AIDS and STDs are outside of our houses. Just be careful what you do in your life.'

The content of young fathers' messages was clear – use protection, rather than abstaining or limiting the number of partners:

Nhlanhla: I won't say abstain but protection is fine, cos when you say abstain you making them even more worse. They would want to know. You know when you tell a child don't do this, don't touch here; he will want to touch there. 'Why are you saying I must not touch here?' It's like that.

Bongani: I would tell him not to have sex without a condom. Because I can't say he shouldn't have sex at all [pause] because these days having sex at a young age is common.

Conclusion

The answers to the multifaceted question 'Why do impoverished young men have multiple sexual partnerships, fail to use condoms and become fathers at a young age?' are related and have been addressed in this chapter by the young fathers who participated in the study. In short, the answers relate to the dearth of services for young men and the failure to engage them in appropriate sex education.

With regard to sexual health services, it is indisputable that services appear to be geared towards women rather than men. Clinics are filled with young women arriving for contraceptive services or ante- or post-natal care; welfare organisations frequently offer 'mother and baby' accommodation, which often restricts visits from young men; hospitals have been found to exclude and marginalise young fathers (Quinton et al. 2002), especially those who are young and 'black' (Kiselica & Sturmer 1993). Kiselica and Sturmer (1993) therefore appropriately talk of the 'mixed messages' we give to young men and women when services are disproportionately allocated to women, but at the same time men are encouraged to take responsibility for their own sexual health and well-being and be a partner in childcare. It is no surprise, therefore, that many young men in this study believed that contraception is the responsibility of women.[27]

As regards sex education, the young men in this study clearly related how sex education failed to engage them at a stage in their lives when they were too playful to listen attentively and too filled with bravado to accept that an unplanned or mistimed child was likely to result from their ignorance and neglect. Furthermore, research has found that while young men are less knowledgeable about sex and relationships than young females (and poor young men even more so),[28] they tend to value and act on the information when it is provided (Blenkinsop et al. 2004). As far as programmes for young fathers are concerned, studies have found them to be effective, especially when young fathers are involved in their design (Lane & Clay 2000; Smith et al. 2001). However, young fathers should not be relied on to solely identify their own needs, since few are able to discern both their need for practical help with child rearing (differentiated by culture)[29] and employment,[30] as well as their need for mental health services to cope with the stress and depression that frequently accompanies mistimed fatherhood (Weinman et al. 2002).

Education about MCPs and condom use is especially key to young men, since each constitutes a behaviour that places young men and their partners at high risk for HIV infection. Young men the world over do not use condoms consistently due to a lack of knowledge and education and because many have a feeling of immunity towards HIV infection (Hansen & Hahn 1990). In a 2007 study in four countries in Africa,[31] it was found that of those 15- to 19-year-olds 'who have had sex in the past year, only 29–47% of females and 42–55% of males used contraceptives the last time' (Biddlecom et al. 2007: 4). In South Africa, the 2003 *Demographic and Health Survey* reported figures for the same age group of 50.4 per cent for young women and 73.8 per cent for young men (DoH 2004: 154). These high rates of condom use among young men are not borne out in the experiences of these young fathers or in their discussion of their peers' condom use. In addition, in a nationally representative Angolan study among 15- to 24-year-olds (Prata et al. 2005), low rates of condom usage similar to those of Biddlecom et al. (2007) were reported, especially among poorly educated youth. The same study also found that young women who equated condom use with *a lack of trust* were less likely to use condoms consistently, while young men who had multiple partners tended to be more consistent condom users.

Recent research (described in Halperin & Epstein 2007) has shown that although African men do not report more lifetime sexual partners than their counterparts elsewhere in the world, it is the fact that

27 What is ironic, of course, is that while young men as partners believe it to be the woman's role to have knowledge of pregnancy and contraception, as brothers and fathers they deny them these preventative services and information (Chikovore et al. 2003).
28 It was found that 'black' youth from low socio-economic backgrounds in the USA had poor knowledge about the risk of pregnancy and basic contraceptive information (Rivara et al. 1985).
29 In a study that asked young Latino, African American and Anglo youth about their need for services for young unmarried fathers, Hendricks (1988) found that needs differed markedly according to culture.
30 In both the literature and the narratives of the young fathers in this study, employment is seen as a panacea to all their problems.
31 A nationally representative study conducted in Burkina Faso, Ghana, Malawi and Uganda.

many are involved in MCPs that seems to place them at higher risk of HIV infection. The authors explain that in southern Africa, men who engage in MCPs increase their risk of acquiring HIV due to the wider sexual network of which they are a part – especially during the highly infectious period that accompanies a new HIV infection, when the virus can spread rapidly given the wide network of stable and ongoing partnerships.[32] Furthermore, Halperin and Epstein argue that young women in southern Africa are not subject to the same sexual surveillance as their counterparts in, for example, northern Africa (and Muslim countries), resulting in both *women* and *men* engaging in MCPs, although at different rates, which further exacerbates the spread of HIV. Biddlecom et al. (2007: 4) report that among 15- to 19-year-olds surveyed in Burkina Faso, Ghana, Uganda and Malawi, 18–26 per cent of young men *and* 6–7 per cent of young women reported having had two or more partners in the past year. In South Africa, according to Shisana et al. (2005: 57), 45.2 per cent of young men reported having two or more current sexual partners, while 28.0 per cent of young women reported two or more partners.

The literature for Africa provides another important piece of data regarding MCPs. In a study of 2 430 youths aged between 15 and 24 in South Africa, it was found that both sexual experience and occurrence of multiple partners were more common among 'black' males living in urban informal settlements (Simbayi et al. 2004: 618) than in other 'racial' groups. What appears to be absent in the literature about MCPs, however, is a possible explanation for why these relationships are so common among 'black' South African men (including youth).

In much of the available literature, the explanation given for young men's practices of multiple partners, along with sexual conquest, lack of condom use and even sexual curiosity from a young age, has been largely attributed to the male role modelling of machismo that many encounter in their communities.[33] And while this is arguably also the case for some of the young fathers in this study, many young men suggest that their behaviour extends beyond that of machismo. With regard to MCPs, Hunter (2005: 389) unravels 'the antecedents of contemporary masculinities' among 'black' men when he describes the notion of an *isoka* (a Zulu man with multiple sexual partners), which arose in response to widespread unemployment in the 1970s. This inhibited men's ability to become *umnumzana* (a household head), which had previously been the dominant expression of manliness in Zulu culture. He argues that 'the high value placed on men seeking multiple-partners increasingly filled the void left by men's inability to become men through previous means', although he concludes that indications are that 'shaken by the huge AIDS deaths, men are betraying increasing doubts about the *isoka* masculinity' (Hunter 2005: 389).

The young men in this study pointed to a further reason for multiple partners, beyond the obvious notion of machismo. In the post-study consultation, the issue of single-parent families was raised. Growing up in these kinds of families meant that attention was 'scarce'; having many young women acted as a substitute for this scarcity of love and attention in their childhood, an assertion borne out by the literature (Winstanley et al. 2002).[34] Attachment theory corroborates this insight. In a study conducted by Ciesla et al. (2004: 108) it was found that young men 'with insecure attachment styles (particularly negative attachment representations of self and fearful attachment) were associated with

---

32 Halperin and Epstein (2007: 21) argue that people need to understand 'the dangers of having more than one longer-term sexual partner at a time, or of having a partner who has more than one longer-term partner…In much of southern Africa, even people with only two lifetime partners – hardly high-risk behaviour by western standards – need to appreciate just how risky that one extra partner can be, for themselves and for others, if the relationships are long-term and concurrent'.

33 'Machismo is considered important in the socialization of boys and encompasses qualities such as masculinity, male dominance, responsibility as the protector of the family, sexual prowess, and physical strength' (Yasui & Dishion 2007: 150). See also Carter et al. (2005).

34 Young men in low socio-economic contexts have higher cumulative psychosocial stressors and display lower levels of intimacy (Winstanley et al. 2002).

having multiple sexual partners [suggesting] that interpersonal issues may play a key role in high-risk sexual behavior'. Yet another study reports that 'the quality of attachments in childhood and adolescence is well known to impact development of critical self-regulatory functions such as emotional definition and control, cognitive self-definition, and interpersonal expectation' (Burk & Burkhart 2003: 487). While the data recorded in these studies do not constitute conclusive evidence of the relationship between poverty, poor attachment pathways and risk behaviours such as MCPs, they do provide a direction for further research. Young men's need for 'attention' and 'possessions' in the face of poverty offers a rich area for further investigation into the psychosocial and mental health needs of young 'black' men, as part of the answer to the question 'What constitutes sexual health and well-being for impoverished youth?' The answer to this question takes on greater significance when one considers that HIV infection among 'black' youth is seven times as high as infection rates among 'coloured' youth and 41 times as high as among 'white' youth (Shisana et al. 2005: 38).

3

CONCLUSIONS AND RECOMMENDATIONS

CHAPTER 7

'Knowing, working, talking and connecting': The crucial needs of young fathers

This study set out to identify those factors and features that are associated with young men's maximum participation in parenting their children, and those forces which hinder their participation. In each of the data chapters (Chapters 3–6) a different feature of young fathers' experience was described, with young men's voices being privileged in each account. Chapter 3 detailed the immense emotion with which the impoverished young fathers who participated in this study described their experiences of becoming and being young fathers. They spoke of their fear of their own and the MOC's parents, of not being able to provide financially, of having educational plans and dreams scuppered, and referred to brief thoughts of terminating the pregnancy but could seldom go through with it. Young men then articulated a strong discourse of responsibility, frequently as a result of having been abandoned by their own fathers. Of course, such a discourse of responsibility is perhaps not surprising since those who participated in the study were those who were facing up to their responsibilities in some form. Yet the strength and passion with which they spoke of their responsibility is not a usual feature of young fathers' research.

They also spoke candidly about the reasons why they became young fathers in the first place and highlighted the ubiquity of alcohol in their lives, which frequently led to having unprotected sex. They also spoke at length about how, from the ages of 14 to 16 especially, they were ignorant about condom use, other forms of contraceptives and general reproductive biology, believing themselves to be too young to father a child. In contrast to popular understanding, young men also spoke of the need for more adult involvement in their lives, and only a few spoke of young women as tempters or wanting children. The chapter clearly shows the enormous contribution that financial pressure plays in terms of hindering young men's involvement with their children – not only because of family expectations, but also because of the way that being unable to provide damages young men's views of themselves and further demotivates them with regard to being involved with their child. At the same time, the chapter flags their sense of responsibility and their desire to be present for their child despite their own experience of failed fathering.

In Chapter 4, young men identified the five types of fathers they had experienced: 'absent fathers', 'financial fathers', 'angry fathers', 'faithless fathers' and 'talking fathers'. They clearly expressed their love of and need for 'talking fathers', followed closely by 'financial fathers'. They spoke of how having an absent, angry or faithless father motivated them to be present in their own child's life, and to talk with, rather than shout at, their children. Although they expressed disapproval of 'faithless' fathers (those who have MCPs), their disapproval did not translate into action to curb their own MCP behaviour (except in a few cases). In addition, the young fathers described, with examples from their own experience, what it means to be a good father – characteristics not only limited to providing financially.

Instead, they also identified the time, care, physical affection and practical involvement a child needs and spoke of the character and 'good reputation' a father ought to have. Somewhat paradoxically, young fathers' description of the all-encompassing features of what it means to be a good father was somewhat overshadowed by their prominent focus on the employment and money needed to be, in their estimation, a truly good father.

Chapter 5 highlighted the high esteem in which young fathers hold their own mothers and asked how mothers could perhaps be empowered to become more involved in their sons' lives, both before and after they become young fathers, without taking over the responsibility of child raising from their sons. It also explored young fathers' experiences with the family of the mother of their child (usually negative) and exposed one of the main reasons for young men's alienation from their children. Finally, this chapter discussed young 'black' men's experiences of damage payments, and the exclusion that young men who are 'boys' rather than 'men' face (especially in amaXhosa culture) when it comes to deciding about childcare arrangements for their child. It offered an example of how young men can engage with elders about the role of culture while still maintaining a respectful participation – one that does not contribute to alienating them from their child.

Finally, in Chapter 6 attention was given to the three main obstacles facing young men (and young fathers) in light of the high incidence of HIV in impoverished communities. Minimal uptake of condom use among young men, their lack of contraceptive knowledge (especially at a young age), and the allure of the connections gained through MCPs are candidly discussed by these young fathers – and they paint a bleak picture. However, this chapter also showed how becoming a young father changes condom and contraceptive use but does little about reducing MCPs. Young fathers referred repeatedly to the limited programmes in their areas, the lack of personal motivation to use those that are available (including voluntary counselling and testing – although some do), the lack of outreach programmes to draw them in, as well as the problems with sex education in school and its almost complete absence in the home environment.

These four chapters, when taken as a whole, provide detailed data regarding the enabling features and hindering factors in ensuring the health of young fathers and their ongoing participation in the lives of their children. These findings are diagrammatically summarised in Figure 7.1. That these young fathers are aware of these factors is further evidence of the articulate and astute manner in which they make recommendations about the help they need and provide advice to other young men who are sexually active and who may also be young fathers.

Young fathers' recommendations about the help they need

Perhaps it is not surprising, given the depth of the data that these young fathers produced over the course of this study, that their recommendations about the help they need are comprehensive and for the most part accurate. Below are young fathers' five recommendations that have been collated from responses to the question 'What needs to be done to help young fathers?'

Communication about sex

Jabu: [Sex education] when it came from your parents it would be – you'd listen…Mostly fathers. You know? I think they might listen, because most guys I know they respect their fathers. I think if their fathers would talk to them, teach them, they would listen.

Vuyo: Tell, the parents of South Africa, *neh*, parents sit with your child at the table, then talk about good things. Like, you can't sleep with a girl without condom.

FIGURE 7.1 *Hindering factors and enabling features affecting young fathers' well-being and participation in parenting*

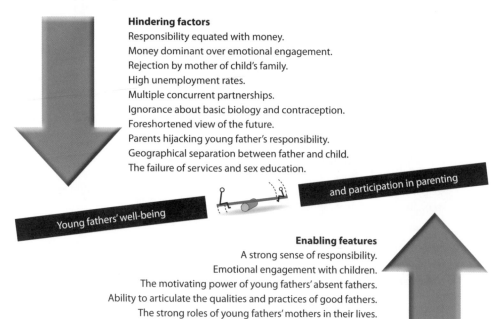

Hindering factors
Responsibility equated with money.
Money dominant over emotional engagement.
Rejection by mother of child's family.
High unemployment rates.
Multiple concurrent partnerships.
Ignorance about basic biology and contraception.
Foreshortened view of the future.
Parents hijacking young father's responsibility.
Geographical separation between father and child.
The failure of services and sex education.

and participation in parenting

Young fathers' well-being

Enabling features
A strong sense of responsibility.
Emotional engagement with children.
The motivating power of young fathers' absent fathers.
Ability to articulate the qualities and practices of good fathers.
The strong roles of young fathers' mothers in their lives.
The effects of being welcomed by mother of child's family.
The desire for sex education and mentoring by peers and family.
Clear aspirations for future involvement with their child.
A clear recognition of the help they need.
HIV testing and post-birth contraceptive use.

Source: Compiled by the authors

Sifiso: Elders shouldn't be shy to talk about sex to young people. I think it's things like that [pause] that can help.

Organised leisure and environmental changes

S'bu: Decrease the number of taverns because they are everywhere.

Marlin: If they – can get those gangsters and drugs out of our township, then it will be much better…They smoke drugs, they don't care, they make children.

Yusuf: If we give them a soccer field, a cricket field, and a netball court for the girls. Look – the kids of today. I know what they like now is Rollerblades and skateboards. The girls also. That's what I think. Things to keep them busy.

Nhlanhla: Now kids are getting pregnant at the ages of [pause] 14, 15 [pause] and what they can be helped by is [pause] give them more activities at school. Don't say to a child you have a paper to go and write at 9 o'clock and you'll finish at 10 o'clock. From 10 o'clock what is that child going to be doing [pause] there is no one at home. After that paper [pause] they should do sport [pause] activities at schools…Let them be activated, you know.

Employment opportunities and help to complete education

Nhlanhla: I think if they gave the young fathers jobs [pause] I think that would be good. Because right now young fathers [pause] most of them, some of them [pause] they don't even work, they stay in town doing robberies, you know…They are not getting educated [pause] they have no jobs, they have no income; so the only way to get income is to go and rob someone. I think [pause] give them something to do. Keep them busy.

Onathi: A stable job…So maybe there can be a programme for young father to be first in the queue to get a job, to get work if there's work being offered.

Lwandile: Some young fathers…were taken out from school to go and work. So, the government can help there to get that child from the work to school again. Because there some other who need to go schooling more further. But they have been forced to come from out from school…If maybe the government could like provide a crèche for the young fathers and mothers – so that they can go to school or go to work!

Psychosocial support using peer educators

Saki: We have to be talking about how to act responsible. That's the only way, that's the only way. We have to be taught how to act responsible…[by] peer educators.

Nhlanhla: Announce that you need young fathers [pause] yah [pause] let them come into a place where we could all fit [pause] and let them know that they are not alone, we are all young fathers…Speak to young people who are not yet fathers, those who are in their teen years…help a few friends to realise what is it like to be a young father.

Fadiel: They must go to the schools – but it must be all the time. If I think back to when I was in school and the programmes. They would come and then leave after two hours, then when I go home I forgot what happened. I don't remember what they did…They must go to the schools all the time. Like every two weeks and keep reminding people to use condoms and about how serious it is. They must tell them how serious it is and life is expensive and having a child is not easy.

Ibrahiem: Maybe put up posters…in Bonteheuwel because there are many, many, many young children that, like, who are mothers and fathers, and in school.

Relationship-building skills

Lonwabo: Firstly, like, I was going to say, like, that at least let them involve me in the child's life from day one. Come to my place…discuss it with me, give me advice, like [pause] how to deal with it, like I don't know! Like how will I, will I support the baby! Be more like – being a father and all that stuff!

Zaid: The way he reacted [MOC's father] – okay, it's normal for a father but he could have reacted differently, man. He could have at least spoke to me after that conversation we had with my mother, them and he could have motivated me and put words in my mind to think what I can do, because I don't have a daddy…he could've tried to be a father to me as well.

At the top of young men's list is the need for educational and employment assistance in various forms. Helping young men return to school, whether through support groups or by providing crèches to enable them to keep their children geographically close while continuing with schooling or studies, are remarkably insightful recommendations. In addition, young men's desire for employment is a structural issue, which our country must address. And while it might not be practical to ensure that young fathers are 'first in the queue for jobs', it might be a good idea to ensure that young men are prepared for employment.

Young men's recognition of the need for help in order to establish better relationships with the family of the mother of their child is a further insightful observation, as is the need for communication about sex and relationships – especially from male members of young men's families. A few young men also made recommendations about virginity testing, helping girls to say no, and stopping the child support grant:

Luxolo: Every weekend or every end of month we can meet in on the fields! Grandmothers, mothers and older sisters…to check! Not to talk! Talk won't help. To check that their children is still a virgin! It's gonna help them! Virgin police! In our communities we call them the virgin police! And it's so that we are hoping it's going to be better! To make the girls afraid to have sex with boys.

Sakhile: I think [pause] if the government could provide money for people who go for virginity testing for instance. And say if a person is still a virgin then she receives money. The money they should earn for being virgins. I think the people would also like the idea of getting money and they won't have sex.

Jabu: Starting from girls [pause]. They should learn to say no.

Vuyo: No, I'm gonna go to Parliament [and tell them], 'No grants for young parents'…I say stop that grant, I think maybe it's better.

These comments are less insightful and have not been included in the list of recommendations since they perpetuate gender stereotypes and double standards, and are not based in fact (the child support grant has not increased teen fertility). Despite the insightfulness of most of these young men's recommendations, they fail to ask for help regarding their proclivity (especially among young 'black' men) for MCPs; the irresponsibility young men display regarding condom use, mainly out of the desire to have maximally fulfilling sex; and the perennial problem of alcohol and other substance use that exacerbates sexual risk taking. In the advice offered to young men who learn they are to become young fathers, however, the issues of condom and substance use do feature, among a litany of other insights.

Advice to young men who are soon to be fathers

The young fathers who participated in this study provided multiple practical guidelines to young men who discover they are about to become fathers or who already are young fathers. Their advice centred on providing for and loving the child rather than denying the child; maintaining a relationship with the mother of the child and her family; seeking out parents' advice and support from the start; and finishing[35] schooling or studies to facilitate getting a good job and being able to provide for their child. Significantly, further advice was not to panic but to 'relax'; having a child at a young age is difficult but 'it's not the end of the world'; to 'slow down' with regards to alcohol, in order to increase their ability to be responsible and not to make the same mistake twice; and to 'condomise'. A list of advice offered, with selected quotes, is reproduced below.

Be responsible

Andile: I would say he must be ready for the coming baby and have the right tools. And not run away and take the responsibility of being a father.

Maintain a relationship with the child's mother and her family

Sakhile: I would tell that he must love the mother of his child before the child is born so that when the child comes, you are having a good relationship.

Yusuf: Don't go wrong with the child's mother. Otherwise they'll experience the same as I have…I am the only one who doesn't see his child.

Sifiso: He shouldn't dump the mother of his child. They must sit down and talk about issues and he should try and think [pause] how is he going to raise the child.

Ibrahiem: Be nice to them [MOC's family] and so on because it's nice when you're in the good books with them. Don't get on their bad side. It makes things difficult.

Speak to parents

Onathi: My advice like – tell your parents that there's something like this. And hear – and hear their advice…because you won't take care of the baby. You have nothing. So, they will take care of the baby.

Xolile: It's better to tell first – your parents – then they will negotiate with the girlfriend's parents – don't wait until they come to your door.

Sabier: They must go to their parents and then tell their parents and she must go tell her parents also. They mustn't wait.

Vuyo: Speak up when you go to negotiate, not to her family – with your parents. Pay *isisu*. But speak to your parents before they go to negotiate.

Prepare for and love the child

S'bu: What I can tell him is that he shouldn't abandon the child. He should try to at least supply the child with necessities.

Fadiel: I would tell him he has to prepare. He has to prepare because he is going to be a father. Everything he do must be for his children.

---

35   Only the 'coloured' young men from Bonteheuwel thought it was more urgent to get a job than to complete their schooling.

Luthando: Ok, my advice is to tell them that if you made someone pregnant you should just look after your kid. If you can't make it with her mother, just look after your kid.

Lwethu: Take care of your child. Love her. Do everything for her, you see? Yah.

Slow down with alcohol and drugs

Lwethu: Yah. I would say, 'Slow down with alcohol.' Cos if you think you, like, you're drinking to forget, there are more problems at the bottom of the bottle, you see?

Marlin: They must grow up and they must leave the things they are involved with because the young fathers love to take drugs. That's the way out for them. That was the way out for me. I couldn't help it.

Don't leave school

Onathi: Finish all your studies, then must get a work as soon as possible. Get a job. That's the most important thing for the baby. If you're jobless, well, you depend on your parents, and that's not good.

S'bu: He shouldn't leave school, because there are lots of people who can help him [pause] if he tells them that he has a child but he is at school.

Get a job

Ibrahiem: I'd tell them, um. Leave the things you are doing and get yourself a job, because having a baby isn't a game and love the mother and the baby.

Sabier: They must go work. They should be able to stand on their own feet. They must find a job.

Don't deny or abandon the child

Tapelo: My advice to them, he must not run away. He must be there for the child no matter he does not have money…He must not be scared because at the time he was having sex he was not scared.

Nhlanhla: Don't run [pause] don't run away…Don't just abandon her.

Lwandile: Firstly, they have to admit the fact they are the fathers.

Zaid: You can't run away from your child or anything, because at the end of the day that child is gonna grow up and he's gonna want to meet you. One or other time. And if he's gonna meet you, he's gonna hate you and then you gonna sit with the guilt.

Xolile: [If you're not sure it's your baby] don't just pay the money in front – wait until the baby is born and you can see – this is my baby.

Don't panic or make the same mistake twice

Dumisani: That person needs help and support. I'll tell him to relax, that's the first thing. Most people when they hear such news they panic and end up doing things like committing suicide.

So they need to calm down. And I will tell him that having a child is not the end of the world.

Sifiso: You have a child okay [pause] but please try not to repeat the same mistake because you've seen what you've put yourself through. Condomise.

In addition, these young fathers had advice for young men to help them *avoid* becoming fathers, including 'using protection', 'don't mix sex and alcohol', understanding the consequences and costs of having a child, and waiting until they have completed school and have a stable job before having a child. The full list of advice is presented below.

Advice to young men to avoid becoming fathers

Use protection

Onathi: Well, my advice to [young guys] is, don't think about it at all [not using condoms]. Condoms are there, so use them.

Luthando: From my experience the guys who don't have a kid now, must stay using a condom, you see. Or if you are not using a condom, go for an injection.

Nhlanhla: To use protection. Use protection…When you become a father…you close some doors. Yah, they should be told to use protection.

Don't mix sex and alcohol

Xolile: Don't even go to the tavern [to have] a one-night stand.

Vuyo: Young people love to drink. Then, you drink, you will do everything. Yes, yes, yes, you forget about condom. So [don't be] careless.

Understand the consequences of having a child

Saki: They are told of the facts but they don't really see the chaos they are creating…I think sex education has to play a role, the most important role in this…Let him [your son] not make the same mistake that you did. You must try give him all the best that you can. Educate him.

Fadiel: They don't understand the risks and the consequences of what will happen. They think having a child is a joke. They don't know it's serious and that there is a lot of responsibility. They don't use condoms because they don't understand how serious it is.

Wait until you have finished school and have a job

Sifiso: If had to advise young guys, I would tell them not to have kids now. I would tell them to rather wait until they finish school, find a job and wait until she/he can see that they alright.

Siya: I think basically they need to stop making babies rather than they not old enough…I am a young parent – and I wouldn't like that to happen to you also!

Vuyo: I can say is not good to get a baby at the young age. Because you can't get everything in your home for the child. And for yourself. Because you've got a child. And then you can't concentrate in your school, like, because you always think about your child.

Creating closer ties through social network interviewing: A possible intervention

For many young fathers, participating in this research study was the first time that they had spoken about their feelings and experiences of being a young father to an objective party (i.e. not parents or partners). Most thanked us for the work we were doing, and were sad when the process was over. The young men approached to conduct social network interviews, read the research report or assist in the analysis were all eager to continue their participation (and more were eager after the debriefing and consultation workshop had showcased the data obtained from the social network interviews). Social network interviews, although used here as case studies, were always intended to test their possible usefulness as an intervention in a wider approach to providing support and services to young men. They worked extremely well after some modification, such as shortening the questions and preparing young fathers for possible responses from those who they interviewed.

The first part of the task consisted of identifying people with whom they should talk. Initially, all the young men chose those with whom it might be easier to talk – people from their own close networks rather than from the MOC's network. After some discussion, this initial barrier was overcome, especially when young men had an opportunity to consider what questions might be asked. They agreed that the questions themselves might help their relationship with the family and network members of the mother of their child, no matter what the relationship might currently be. When reporting back to a researcher following his social network interviews, Lwandile commented:

Lwandile: It does give them [the people he interviewed] a chance to give us a kick, but I can take one kick and get it over with – then, uhmm, hear some of the other things they have to say [pause]. Like also there's a chance for them to say what they could have done, and they never did do to help. So yah, it's a good thing. I was still scared, but I did it, yah.

Lwandile was quite right in identifying two types of questions: the first that allowed people to speak their mind and possibly clear the air, and the second that tried to move forward in a mutually helpful manner. Table 7.1 provides a more detailed analysis of the intention of each question. Social network interview questions begin by allowing the respondent to recall the occasion and reflect on their response and advice at the time (questions 1 and 2). Questions 3 and 4 allow respondents to evaluate young fathers' performance and invite constructive criticism. Although uncomfortable for young fathers, these questions assist in building the relationship and establishing rapport. Question 5 proceeds to a specific analysis of the role of culture (both positive and negative) in young fatherhood, while questions 6 to 8 return to more constructive advice for young fathers – including a dispassionate analysis of why young fathers lose contact with their children over time.

Of course, in considering how social network interviews might be used as an intervention, it is also useful to analyse which people young men chose to interview and why. The four young men who agreed to conduct these interviews are too small a sample upon which to base firm conclusions, but they do provide some insight. Of the possible list provided to them (see Appendix 1), their choices were driven first by fear and then by access.

TABLE 7.1 *The eight social network interview questions with corresponding aims*

Question	Aim
1. Do you remember how you responded when I told you that I was going to be a father? What did you say at the time? What did you think at the time?	Opportunity to recollect and talk about feelings and thoughts which may or may not have been expressed at the time.
2. What advice did you give me at the time?	Focus on advice rather than merely on emotions.
3. How do you think I should have behaved differently since hearing I was going to become a father?	Inviting constructive evaluation, especially if a significant period of time has elapsed since the news of the pregnancy or birth of the child.
4. What kind of father do you think I have been since the time my baby was born?	
5. In what way do you think our culture has helped me to be a good father? In what way do you think our culture has stopped me from being a good father?	More objective evaluation, especially around issues of culture such as *isisu, hlonipha, ukudliwa* and even perhaps *ilobolo*, as well as the role of young men in deciding about care and support for their children (especially if they are still *inkwenkwe* rather than *indoda*).
6. What role do you think a young father should play in the life of their children – if they are not married to the mother? Should this role change over time, for example when the child is newly born, when s/he is 10, when s/he is 18 years old?	Inviting some analysis that will also provoke young men's own self-evaluation and future planning.
7. Why do you think young men often lose contact with their children over the years?	
8. What advice do you have for me about being a young father for the future?	

Lwandile chose those closest to him in his own network (including his grandfather and uncle who had cared for him since the age of seven after his mother's death) as well as a close friend and a cousin who he had grown up with. His self-confessed fear led him to avoid speaking to either of the parents of the mother of his child, choosing instead to speak to her uncle and male cousin (in addition to two of her close friends). Even in choosing a cousin and uncle, he told of how he ensured they were well lubricated with alcohol before he dared to interview them, saying that he did not think they would have spoken to him without it.

Vuyo, on the other hand, steered completely clear of any members of the mother of his child's network and limited his interviews to his mother, a 'stand-in' father (his was absent), his older brother and a close friend. Onathi expanded his selection of interview candidates to include the mother of his child's grandmother and aunt, in addition to the mother of his child, a teacher and an uncle. He had also arranged to interview his father, but tragedy intervened when his father was shot and killed on the day he had planned the interview – a victim of a car hijacking in Gugulethu. Onathi's more expansive choice reflected his own confidence, his status as a man in the amaXhosa community and the fact that he was in good standing with the MOC's family regarding damage payments and his ongoing presence and support for the child.

Siya's choices of interview subjects further (and bravely) expanded on Onathi's and included both the parents of the mother of his child, as well as the mother of his child, her sister, and his own grandmother, father and two close friends. His two interviews with the MOC's mother and father have already been considered in Chapter 5. It is clear that the interview itself was a helpful next step in their relationship. Siya's account of their relationship (certainly with the father) was more positive than the interviews portrayed. Siya's comment after the interview was that he had 'learnt a lot' and that it had taken their relationship to 'another level'.

Social network interviews appear to contribute to young men's desire to expand and deepen their relationship with the mother of their child as well as her family and social network. In Siya's case, his interview with his father, who was absent during Siya's childhood and only recently re-emerged and entered into a relationship with him, was a poignant reunion and an important part of Siya's maturing as a young father. Following is the interview in its entirety, as an example of the depth of disclosure that these simple interviews evoked.

Siya: Do you remember how you responded when I told you that I was going to be a father? What did you say at the time? What did you think at the time?

Father: I do remember, I just got very disappointed in myself and I knew that deep inside I was wrong. I have nothing more to say by the word of mouth to you that can express the way I feel at heart. And what happened is part of me and my way of treating you.

Siya: What advice did you give me at the time?

Father: As I told you, I want to be that father figure in your life once again. And I know I failed as a father to you, but know you can change that to your strength. Be what I failed to be in your life, and be the dad you needed me to be in your life.

Siya: How do you think I should have behaved differently since hearing I was going to become a father?

Father: As I told you, I know that I may have no say in your life for now. And you must acknowledge the fact that you do not have to do what I did in your life, and you end up doing it to your own child's life.

Siya: What kind of father do you think I have been since the time my baby was born?

Father: That I cannot answer, as I have not been involved in your life that much. But I do believe you have tried your best – and may you continue.

Siya: In what way do you think our culture has helped me to be a good father? In what way do you think our culture has stopped me from being a good father?

Father: Look, I told you that I cannot say that much about you because I know what I did back then.

Siya: What role do you think a young father should play in the life of their children – if they are not married to the mother? Should this role change over time, for example when the child is newly born, when s/he is 10, when s/he is 18 years old?

Father: I know that as a young father you should do what I did to you in an opposite manner. I would tell them to do what they will not want their children to hate them for.

Siya: Why do you think young men often lose contact with their children over the years?

Father: Now that I can answer because that is what happened to you and me. You see, sometime in life you can think and plan your life to the end of time, but life is like a plastic ball: You may kick it with assurance that it will go where your intentions are, but it will meet wind along the way, and then the direction will change from there – going to another side. Now that is life, my boy.

Siya: What advice do you have for me about being a young father in the future?

Father: My boy, stand up, look up, and live your life to the point that your child wants to thank you for what you have done in his/her life. That is what I can tell you, my boy.

When considering these young men's social network interviews, it is apparent that they have at least two further uses when working with vulnerable or hard-to-reach populations. First, they provide rich data for studies such as this one. Three examples illustrate the point: (1) In Onathi's interview with his teacher, in answering the question about why young fathers lose contact with their children, his teacher speaks frankly about the temptation of other women, including in his own situation as a married man; (2) Interviews with the mother of Onathi's and Siya's child reflect the current status of their relationship, as well as the sense of vulnerability the young woman feels in their relationship; and (3) Vuyo's interaction with his close friend shows how young men reflect on the possibility of an abortion, and supports earlier analysis that becoming a young father is frequently considered a kind of competition among young men. His friend says, 'I – actually – I was really surprised. I thought, "Oh no, my friend now is going to be father, although I don't even have one baby." *Eish* – then I thought that, you know, I should get mine one.'

Second, these social network interviews provide a means of learning for young fathers that they might otherwise not have received. Reading Vuyo's interview with his close friend provided a good example of the peer assessment that is possible between two young men:

Vuyo's friend: As your closest friend, uh, because I've been spending a lot of time with you – [I can see that] you don't take care of your baby. You're very – sometimes you become irresponsible – you're there by your girlfriend's place instead of doing what you must do to keep contact with your baby [Vuyo is not in a relationship with the mother of his child].

Vuyo's friend continues to commiserate with how the mother of Vuyo's child's family treats Vuyo, mainly due to his 'struggle financially', yet admonishes him to be more responsible and to sacrifice time with his current girlfriend for time with his child. Although there was not an opportunity to ascertain Vuyo's response to such candid peer evaluation, evidence would point to the fact that young men might hear such admonition better from a peer than from a parent or even from the mother of their child.

Lwandile's discussion with his grandfather and the MOC's uncle, especially around culture, is mirrored in Siya's and Onathi's interviews with older male members of their networks. Lwandile's grandfather and the MOC's uncle openly admit that culture plays a role in protecting the young man, but also contributes to alienating the young father from his child and the mother of his child:

Grandfather: The culture forced us to stand for you at the beginning when the family had to tell you that you make their child heavy [pregnant]. So they could not talk with you because of your age. That's how the culture made you a good father. But it also made you a bad father because of excluding you in many things that take place in the process of this.

MOC's uncle: The culture has helped you in a way that you did not have to work on your own. It forced your family to help you with the problem. And the culture stopped you to be a good father when you were not allowed to come to the family alone, whereas your child is there…In our culture there is no role a young father can play. It's only his family that can do anything for the sake of the child. It's only the family that can do anything…The culture can be one of the causes of losing the contact because if you are a young father sometimes you have no say. So there is someone to decide for you.

For a young father to hear this from the people who guard and enforce cultural traditions, customs and rules must have a profound effect, especially since these young men had already vented their frustration (albeit to an impartial researcher) about the obstacles that cultural traditions create. It would seem that such candour on the part of the older men in their lives must invite further discussion, and could have the effect of young men feeling more empowered and perhaps even more determined to adapt some of these traditions so that they enjoy their benefits without falling victim to some of their overwhelming burdens. Siya's insistence on going to tell the mother of his child's parents, rather than leaving everything up to the cultural code of male family members negotiating with each other without the young father having any say, is one clear example of how this can be achieved.

These uses of social network interviews make them an obvious recommendation for interventions and research among young fathers and other vulnerable groups. Social network interviews appear to have the potential to be a didactic tool, enabling young men to learn things about their own behaviour and circumstances; to provide insight into their experiences from a research point of view; and to allow them to strengthen (or develop) relationships with the family and friends of the mother of their child. Accordingly, while young fathers' perspectives are un(der)researched and important, how young men experience fatherhood is only one half of the picture that needs to be understood in order for successful interventions to be designed. The second half of the study – young men's social network interviews – were also crucial in helping young men to process and plan for any future (and beneficial) involvement in the lives of their children. For this reason, while the second phase of this study has been limited, it has the potential to provide a model for future interventions. Based on the outcomes of this study, it is proposed that an intervention be piloted that encourages young men to meet with other young fathers in small discussion groups and to use social network interviews as a means for strengthening their social networks and supporting their fathering efforts. These discussion groups can be convened at schools, churches, youth centres or on street corners.

Recommendations for further study

As rich and as nuanced as the data in this study have been, each chapter describing the phenomenon of young fatherhood in the context of poverty provides fuel for further research. The disproportionate shame and fear described by (especially) isiXhosa young men in Chapter 3 warrants further investigation and theorising. Young men's involvement with their children over time (Chapter 4) could be the source of a fruitful longitudinal study, especially given that the literature is somewhat contradictory on the topic and also tracks young men for a mere five years after the birth of their child. In Chapter 5 (and again in this chapter) the recommendation of using social network interviewing as a method for intervention needs wider implementation and demonstration of its efficacy or otherwise. Findings on young fathers' lack of motivation for using the limited programmes available (Chapter 6) ought to be the subject of ethnographic research (most useful through participant observation and perhaps involving young fathers themselves as researchers).

In addition, while much research has been done on adolescent-friendly reproductive health services, a focus on adolescent male-friendly services is sorely needed to mitigate the effects of the HIV pandemic on young sexually active (and impoverished) men. Related to the provision of services ought to be an investigation into what actually happens in sex education classrooms and how younger adolescents can be helped to 'tune in' to the information they need about contraception, pregnancy and relationships before they stumble ignorantly into fatherhood. Further related to sex education and services is the need for peer education and support to be supplemented with adult knowledge so that young men do not perpetuate inaccurate information or unhelpful cultural or gender stereotypes (especially in regard to who ought to be responsible for contraception or saying no to sex, and a need to separate condom use from issues of trust and fidelity). Finally, young men's predilection for MCPs needs to be addressed in the light of the failed attachment pathways many experience as a result of growing up in stressed and impoverished communities and families.

Teenage *tatas* (fathers) face multiple challenges to remaining involved with their children. However, if the young fathers in this study reflect the experiences of the multitude of young fathers from impoverished communities who do want to make the effort to remain involved as loving and present parents, then this study has provided a textured and grainy portrait of some of the markers that ought to be operationalised into policy and programmatic interventions. Young fathers' stories need to become known and narrow stereotypes abandoned. Young fathers need help accessing meaningful employment, although this is only one aspect of what it takes to be a father. Young fathers need to be helped to talk – to each other, to service providers and to educators – in order to address attachment and mental health issues that reduce risk. Sex education and services for young men need a radical overhaul. Young men's own agency in developing strong social networks needs to be encouraged, and male family members and peers need to take greater (and perhaps joint) responsibility for ensuring that these teenage *tatas* grow up to be respected *babas* in their communities and in the lives of their cherished children. Finally, young fathers need interventions that will help them make and retain lifelong connections with the mother of their child and her family, regardless of the nature of their romantic relationship, to ensure that they become the 'talking' and present fathers they admire and to which they aspire.

Appendix 1   Interview schedules

First interview with young fathers

- *Check consent form signed and information sheet understood*
- *Check pseudonym chosen*
- *Check on availability and date for second interview*

1. Tell me a little about yourself – your age, working, schooling, where you live, etc.
2. Tell me about the circumstances surrounding when you became a father.
   Probe: When, what happened, was it planned?
3. How did you respond when you found out your girlfriend/partner was pregnant?
   Probe: Feelings – what did you feel?; Actions – what was the first thing you did, what else did you do, who did you tell?
4. How do you feel about being a father now?
5. How are you involved in the life of your child? Why? How would you like to be involved, now and in the future? [See table on the next page.]
   Probe: Engaged, somewhat engaged, disengaged?
6. Complete checklist on the next page. Ask: What was your relationship with the mother of your child at the time the baby was conceived? By the time the baby was born? What is your current relationship with the mother of your child?
   Prompt: Did you have any other sexual partners/girlfriends when you were together with the mother of your child?
7. Do you know your HIV status? That of your child? The mother of your child?
8. What practices have you been involved in around this baby?
   Prompt: Cultural: damage payments, ancestors; Religious: baptism, cleansing rituals.
9. *Distribute copies of the 'three field map' to young men and ask them to complete it.* Ask: Who have been ALL the people who have been involved around you and your baby?
   Prompt: People you've spoken to, asked advice from, helped you, seen you (absolutely everyone you can think of).
   Ask participant to draw it on a blank sheet of paper – and to include himself and his baby in the diagram.
   Prompt: At home, friends, in the wider community, school, church, clinic?
10. What advice did each of these people give you when you first heard you were going to become a father? Along the way?
11. If I were to meet them and talk to them about your experience of being a young father, what do you think they would say to me about you?
12. What advice would you like to give to these people about how they treated you? If I had a chance to meet them, what questions would you like me to ask them?
13. How would you treat your son/daughter if they came and told you they got (someone) pregnant while they were still very young?
14. What would you do to help your son/daughter avoid getting (someone) pregnant in the first place?

When your baby was conceived		Together as a couple (exclusive/not exclusive)
		Casual partners (having sex but not exclusive)
		Other (describe)
When your baby was born		Together as a couple (exclusive/not exclusive)
		Casual partners (still having sex but not exclusive)
		Friends (but not having sex)
		No longer see each other
		Only see each other about coming baby
		Other (describe)
In the year(s) after your baby arrived		Together as a couple (exclusive/not exclusive)
		Casual partners (still having sex but not exclusive)
		Friends (but not having sex)
		No longer see each other
		Only see each other about baby
		Other (describe)
Today		Together as a couple (exclusive/not exclusive)
		Casual partners (still having sex but not exclusive)
		Friends (but not having sex)
		No longer see each other
		Only see each other about baby
		Other (describe)
In the future		Together as a couple (exclusive/not exclusive)
		Casual partners (still having sex but not exclusive)
		Friends (but not having sex)
		No longer see each other
		Only see each other about baby
		Other (describe)

Second interview with young fathers

- *Check travel expenses and receipt*
- *Check guardians consent form signed if under 18*
- *Six cards and koki per participant*

1. Many young men deny they are fathers and simply run away. How come you decided to admit that you were the father of this child? What's different about you?
2. Tell me some more about your child.
   Probe: Whose surname does the baby have? Is this important? What is your relationship with him or her like now?
3. How, in what ways, has having this child changed your life? (What's different in your life since you've had this child?)
   Probe: Describe a typical weekend before the baby arrived, and now?
4. How would you like your child to describe you, or remember you one day when you're no longer around?
5. What makes someone a good father? In what ways are you a good father?
   Probe: What does a good father do, how does a good father speak to his child, how does a good father behave around his child?
6. What/who has helped you to be a good father?
7. What/who has gotten in the way of you being a good father?
8. Complete cards: Give young man 6 cards and ask them to list three people/things who have been the most helpful/least helpful in their experience of being a young father. Ensure that they rank them 1–3 for each MOST helpful/LEAST helpful.
9. Why do you think young people become parents at such a young age?
10. How do you think they can be helped in this experience of being a young parent? How do you think they can be helped to avoid becoming parents at a young age?
    Probe: How can sex education be improved? Do you know of any programmes for young fathers/young parents? Have you ever received any formal help with being a young father?
11. What advice do you have for young men who learn they are going to become fathers?

Social network interviews done by young fathers

- *Choose 3–5 of the following people from each column to interview (use appended questions):*

People in your network		People in the mother of your child's network	
Teacher		Mother of child's mother	
Community leader		Mother of child's father	
Close friend 1		Mother of child's male cousin (cousin brother)	
Close friend 2		Mother of child's female cousin (cousin sister)	
Sister		Mother of child's sister	
Brother		Mother of child's brother	
Mother		Mother of child's aunt	

People in your network		People in the mother of your child's network	
Father		Mother of child's uncle	
Male cousin (cousin brother)		Mother of child's grandmother	
Female cousin (cousin sister)		Mother of child's grandfather	
Grandmother		Mother of child's close friend 1	
Grandfather		Mother of child's close friend 2	
Aunt		Mother of child's teacher	
Uncle		Mother of child's nurse from clinic	
Mother of child (MOC)		Mother of child's community leader	

1. Do you remember how you responded when I told you that I was going to be a father? What did you say at the time? What did you think at the time?
2. What advice did you give me at the time?
3. How do you think I should have behaved differently since hearing I was going to become a father?
4. What kind of father do you think I have been since the time my baby was born?
5. In what way do you think our culture has helped me to be a good father? In what way do you think our culture has stopped me from being a good father?
6. What role do you think a young father should play in the life of their children if they are not married to the mother? Should this role change over time, for example when the child is newly born, when s/he is 10, when she is 18 years old?
7. Why do you think young men often lose contact with their children over the years?
8. What advice do you have for me about being a young father for the future?

Appendix 2   Consent forms

For young fathers

CONSENT FORM – Young father

Young Fathers' Research Project

Hello. My name is _____ and I am from the Human Sciences Research Council. The Human Sciences Research Council is a national research organisation, and we are conducting research about young men's experience of becoming fathers while teenagers. While it's not going to help you now, it is a really important project to make sure that young men's voices, opinions and thoughts are heard and recorded for when schools, youth organisations and government departments plan programmes for young fathers.

What role can you play in the research?

We have invited you to be an interview participant because you are a young father. We will be interviewing a number of young fathers. After combining all the responses, we hope to learn more about young fathers' experiences. This will help us make useful recommendations toward programmes for young fathers in future.

What does the research involve?

The study will run from June to November 2008 and there are important ways for you to be involved:

- Volunteer to speak to me individually (twice) about your experiences as a young father at a time we both agree, for about an hour each time – and respect the times of meetings we make.
- Introduce me to some of the people in your life who were involved in and affected by you becoming a young father, and only if you feel comfortable doing so.
- Participate in a group discussion with other young fathers (if you'd like to) at the end of the project to discuss how you've found your involvement in this study.
- Talk with me about some of the things I will be saying in my report and tell me whether you agree or disagree with my conclusions.
- Give me permission to record our discussions.

How will your involvement in the research affect you?

While you might find it a little uncomfortable talking about such a private experience, you might also find that it helps to talk about it. Your involvement in the discussions will be completely voluntary. I will make sure that your costs for transport and meals are paid on the days you participate. You may choose not to answer any of the questions I ask you and may withdraw from the discussion (and any further participation) at any time. Nothing you say will be right or wrong. I will be interested in everything you tell me.

We will respect your privacy, but have to obey the law

Your responses will remain confidential and nothing you tell me will be shared with anyone in a way in which you will be identified. I will ask you to choose a made-up name for the purposes of this project. However, please note that I cannot guarantee that the other people in the group discussion will keep your responses confidential.

I also need to let you know that if you are under 18 years old and you tell me anything about you or others being mistreated in any way, I will have to share this information with someone who can help you (the Commissioner of Child Welfare).

I have included the phone numbers of Childline, Stop Gender Violence and the national AIDS Helpline who you can call if you are being hurt or harmed in any way, or if you have questions you need to discuss. If you prefer, I will gladly recommend someone you can talk to about any uncomfortable feelings you have after talking to me about being a young father, and by organising a group discussion with other young fathers at the end of the project.

What will happen to the information?

If you agree to talk to us, and you give us permission to do so, the discussions will be tape-recorded. As soon as we have made a transcript of the tape recording, we will make sure that no names of actual people appear in the transcript. The tape recording will be destroyed, and the transcript will be stored in a locked filing system at the Human Sciences Research Council. Only the researchers will have access to the transcript.

Your permission to participate

If you would like to participate in the Young Fathers study you need to sign a consent form as confirmation of your permission. If you are under 18 years of age, one of your parents or your legal guardian also needs to sign a form giving permission, which I will let you have.

Please do not hesitate to contact me if you have any further questions.

Questions and contact numbers

Any study-related questions, problems or emergencies should be directed to the following people:

Dr Sharlene Swartz at email address: sswartz@hsrc.ac.za or telephone 021 466 7874
Professor Arvin Bhana at email address: abhana@hsrc.ac.za or telephone 031 242 5502

Questions about your rights as a study participant, comments or complaints about the study may also be presented to the Research Ethics Committee, Human Sciences Research Council, Cape Town, or by telephone to **0800 212 123** (this is a toll-free call if made from a landline telephone; otherwise cellphone rates apply).

If you need to talk to someone about anything that is worrying you or if you are being hurt in any way please call:

Childline	**0800 055 555**
Stop Gender Violence Helpline	**0800 150 150**
AIDS Helpline	**0800 012 322**

All of these numbers are free calls from landlines; otherwise cellphone rates apply.

CONSENT FORM – Young father

Young Fathers' Research Project

I hereby agree to participate in research regarding young fathers in South Africa.

I understand that I am participating freely and without being forced in any way to do so.

I understand that this is a research project whose purpose is not necessarily to benefit me personally.

I also understand that I can stop my participation at any point should I not want to continue and that this decision will not in any way affect me negatively.

I have received the telephone number of a person to contact should I need to speak about any issues that may arise in this interview.

_____   _____

Signature of Participant   Date

_____   _____

Signature of Witness   Date

I hereby give permission for the interview to be recorded.

_____   _____

Signature of Participant   Date

_____   _____

Signature of Witness   Date

For members of social networks

CONSENT FORM – Social network member

Young Fathers' Research Project

Hello. My name is _____ and I am the researcher responsible for the Young Fathers project currently being run by the Human Sciences Research Council (HSRC). The Human Sciences Research Council is a national research organisation, and we are conducting research about young men's experience of becoming fathers, including their relationships with friends, family and community members. We are doing so in order to ensure that young men's voices, opinions, and thoughts, as well as those of their immediate family and friends, are heard and recorded for when schools, youth organisations and government departments plan programmes for young fathers.

What does the research involve?

The study will run from June to November 2008. I would really like you to participate in this study by agreeing to speak to the young father whom you know who will be asking you a few short questions.

How will your involvement in the research affect you?

The discussion will last around half an hour. Please understand that your participation is voluntary. You are completely free to withdraw from the study at any time you like, and you can choose not to answer any of the questions. However, I would really appreciate it if you do share your thoughts and experiences.

What will happen to the information?

If you agree to participate, we would also like your permission to tape-record the discussions. As soon as I have made a transcript of the tape recording, I will make sure that no names of actual people appear in the transcript. The tape recording will be destroyed, and the transcript will be stored in a locked filing system at the Human Sciences Research Council. Only researchers will have access to the transcript.

If you would like to participate in the Young Fathers study you need to sign the attached consent form as confirmation of your permission.

Questions and contact numbers

Any study-related questions, problems or emergencies should be directed to Dr Sharlene Swartz at email address: sswartz@hsrc.ac.za or telephone 021 466 7874. Questions about your rights as a study participant, comments or complaints about the study may also be presented to the Research Ethics Committee, Human Sciences Research Council, Cape Town, or by telephone to **0800 212 123** (this is a toll-free call if made from a landline telephone; otherwise cellphone rates apply). If you need to talk to someone about anything that is worrying you or if you are being hurt in any way please call:

Stop Gender Violence Helpline   **0800 150 150**

AIDS Helpline   **0800 012 322**

All of these numbers are free calls from landlines; otherwise cellphone rates apply.

CONSENT FORM – Social network member

Young Fathers' Research Project

I hereby agree to participate in research regarding young fathers in South Africa.

I understand that I am participating freely and without being forced in any way to do so.

I understand that this is a research project whose purpose is not necessarily to benefit me personally.

I also understand that I can stop my participation at any point should I not want to continue and that this decision will not in any way affect me negatively.

I have received the telephone number of a person to contact should I need to speak about any issues that may arise in this study.

_____   _____

Signature of Participant   Date

_____   _____

Signature of Witness   Date

I hereby give permission for the interview to be recorded.

_____   _____

Signature of Participant   Date

_____   _____

Signature of Witness   Date

References

Allen WD & Doherty WJ (1996) The responsibilities of fatherhood as perceived by African American teenage fathers. *Families in Society* 77(3): 142–155

Anderson E (1993a) Sex codes and family life among poor inner-city youths. In WJ Wilson (ed.) *The ghetto underclass: Social science perspectives*. Thousand Oaks, CA: Sage Publications

Anderson E (1993b) *Streetwise: Race, class and change in urban community*. Chicago: University of Chicago Press

Anthony I & Smith DL (1994) Adolescent fathers: A positive acknowledgment in the school setting. *Social Work in Education* 16(3): 179–184

Armstrong P, Lekezwa B & Siebrits K (2008) *Poverty in South Africa: A profile based on recent household surveys*. Stellenbosch Economic Working Papers 04/08. Stellenbosch: Department of Economics and the Bureau for Economic Research at the University of Stellenbosch

Baker J, Lynch K, Cantillon S & Walsh J (2004) *Equality: From theory to action*. New York: Palgrave Macmillan

Barret RL & Robinson BE (1981) Teenage fathers: A profile. *Personnel & Guidance Journal* 60(4): 226–228

Barret RL & Robinson BE (1982) Teenage fathers: Neglected too long. *Social Work* 27(6): 484–488

Biddlecom AE, Hessburg L, Singh S, Bankole A & Darabi L (2007) *Protecting the next generation in sub-Saharan Africa: Learning from adolescents to prevent HIV and unintended pregnancy*. New York: Guttmacher Institute

Blenkinsop S, Wade P, Benton T, Gnald M & Schagen S (2004) *Evaluation of the Apause SRE Programme*. Available at http://www.nfer.ac.uk/research-areas/pims-data/summaries/srp-evaluation-of-the-a-pause-sex-and-relationships-education-programme.cfm. Accessed on 15 January 2009

Breslin M (1997) Adult partners of teenage mothers frequently have an inadequate education. *Family Planning Perspectives* 29(5): 238–239

Breslin M (1998) Delinquency and young fatherhood share some, but not all, risk factors. *Family Planning Perspectives* 30(3): 152

Broadfield CS (2006) *Teen fathers: Attachment based on fatherhood skills gained from their father's attitude*. Dissertation, Capella University. ProQuest Dissertation and Theses DAI-B 66/08, p. 4532. Available at http://gateway.proquest.com/openurl%3furl_ver=Z39.88-2004%26res_dat=xri:pqdiss%26rft_val_fmt=info:ofi/fmt:kev:mtx:dissertation%26rft_dat=xri:pqdiss:3185666. Accessed on 15 January 2009

Bronfenbrenner U (1986) Ecology of the family as a context for human development: Research perspectives. *Developmental Psychology* 22(6): 723–742

Bronfenbrenner U (1992) Ecological systems theory. In R Vasta (ed.) *Six theories of child development*. London: Jessica Kingsley Publishers

Bucklin JE (1999) Teen fathers' levels of involvement with their children and their levels of empathy, parental stress, and attachment to parents and peers. Dissertation, California School of Professional Psychology

Bunting L & McAuley C (2004) Research review: Teenage pregnancy and parenthood: The role of fathers. *Child & Family Social Work* 9(3): 295–303

Burk LR & Burkhart BR (2003) Disorganized attachment as a diathesis for sexual deviance. *Aggression and Violent Behavior* 8: 487–511

Carter RT, Williams B, Juby HL & Buckley TR (2005) Racial identity as mediator of the relationship between gender role conflict and severity of psychological symptoms in black, Latino, and Asian men. *Sex Roles* 53(7/8): 473–486

Chikovore J, Nystrom L, Lindmark G & Ahlberg BM (2003) Denial and violence: Paradoxes in men's perspectives to premarital sex and pregnancy in rural Zimbabwe. *African Sociological Review* 7(1): 53–72

Ciesla JA, Roberts JE & Hewitt RG (2004) Adult attachment and high-risk sexual behavior among HIV-positive patients. *Journal of Applied Social Psychology* 34(1): 108–124

Coleman J & Dennison C (1998) Teenage parenthood. *Children & Society* 12(4): 306–314

Colman A (1993) Teenage fathers tend to vanish. *Youth Studies Australia* 12–15(4): 12

Cruzat C & Aracena M (2006) Meaning of fatherhood in male adolescents of the south-east area of Santiago. *Psykhe* 15(1): 29–44

Davies SL, Dix ES, Rhodes SD, Harrington KF, Frison S & Willis L (2004) Attitudes of young African American fathers toward early childbearing. *American Journal of Health Behavior* 28(5): 418–425

Dearden KA, Hale CB & Woolley T (1995) The antecedents of teen fatherhood: A retrospective case-control study of Great Britain youth. *American Journal of Public Health* 85(4): 551–554

Devault A, Milcent M-P, Ouellet F, Laurin I, Jauron M & Lacharite C (2008) Life stories of young fathers in contexts of vulnerability. *Fathering: A Journal of Theory, Research, & Practice about Men as Fathers* 6(3): 226–248

DoH (Department of Health, South Africa) (2002) *South Africa Demographic and Health Survey 1998: Full report.* Pretoria: Department of Health

DoH (2004) *South African Demographic and Health Survey 2003: Preliminary report.* Pretoria: Department of Health

DoSD (Department of Social Development, South Africa) (2006) *Report on incentive structures of social assistance grants in South Africa.* Pretoria: Department of Social Development

Edwards SD, Borsten GF, Nene LM & Kunene ST (1986) Urbanization and changing perceptions of responsibilities among African fathers. *Journal of Psychology: Interdisciplinary and Applied* 120(5): 433–438

Elster AB & Hendricks L (1986) Stresses and coping strategies of adolescent fathers. In AB Elster & ME Lamb (eds) *Adolescent fatherhood.* Hillsdale, NJ: Lawrence Erlbaum Associates

ESRC (Economic and Social Research Council) (1997) *Twenty-something in the 1990s: Getting on, getting by, getting nowhere.* Research brief. Swindon: ESRC

Fagan J, Bernd E & Whiteman V (2007) Adolescent fathers' parenting stress, social support, and involvement with infants. *Journal of Research on Adolescence* 17(1): 1–22

Florsheim P, Moore D, Zollinger L, MacDonald J & Sumida E (1999) The transition to parenthood among adolescent fathers and their partners: Does antisocial behavior predict problems in parenting? *Applied Developmental Science* 3(3): 178–191

Freeman LC, White DR & Romney AK (1989) *Research methods in social network analysis.* Fairfax, VA: George Mason University Press

Friemel T (2007) *Applications of social network analysis: Proceedings of the 3rd conference on applications of social network analysis 2006.* Konstanz: UVK Verlagsgesellschaft

Fry PS & Trifiletti RJ (1983) Teenage fathers: An exploration of their developmental needs and anxieties and the implications for clinical–social intervention and services. *Journal of Psychiatric Treatment & Evaluation* 5(2): 219–227

Futris TG & Schoppe-Sullivan SJ (2007) Mothers' perceptions of barriers, parenting alliance, and adolescent fathers' engagement with their children. *Family Relations* 56(3): 258–269

Giddens A & Birdsall K (2001) *Sociology* (4th edition). Cambridge: Polity

Glikman H (2004) Low-income young fathers: Contexts, connections, and self. *Social Work* 49(2): 195–206

Gohel M, Diamond JJ & Chambers CV (1997) Attitudes toward sexual responsibility and parenting: An exploratory study of young urban males. *Family Planning Perspectives* 29(6): 280–283

Goodman L (1961) Snowball Sampling. Annual Mathematics Statistics 32(1): 148–170

Halperin D & Epstein H (2007) Why is HIV prevalence so severe in southern Africa? The role of multiple concurrent partnerships and lack of male circumcision: Implications for HIV prevention. *Southern African Journal of HIV Medicine* 26: 19–25

Hansen WB & Hahn GL (1990) Perceived personal immunity: Beliefs about susceptibility to AIDS. *Journal of Sex Research* 27(4): 622–628

Hardy JB & Duggan AK (1988) Teenage fathers and the fathers of infants of urban, teenage mothers. *American Journal of Public Health* 78(8): 919–922

Harrison D (2008) Three ways to reduce teen pregnancy in South Africa. Paper presented at the HSRC Youth Policy Initiative Pregnancy Roundtable, 6 March, Pretoria

Hendricks LE (1988) Outreach with teenage fathers: A preliminary report on three ethnic groups. *Adolescence* 23(91): 711–720

Herzog MJ, Umaña-Taylor AJ, Madden-Derdich DA & Leonard SA (2007) Adolescent mothers' perceptions of fathers' parental involvement: Satisfaction and desire for involvement. *Family Relations* 56(3): 244–257

Himonga C (2001) Implementing the rights of the child in African legal systems: The Mthembu journey in search of justice. *International Journal of Children's Rights* 9(2): 89–122

Hollander D (1996) Teenage fathers may play larger role in child care than is often thought. *Family Planning Perspectives* 28(2): 85–86

Hunter M (2005) Cultural politics and masculinities: Multiple partners in historical perspective in KwaZulu-Natal. *Culture, Health & Sexuality* 7(4): 389–403

Hunter M (2006) Fathers without Amandla: Zulu-speaking men and fatherhood. In L Richter & R Morrell (eds) *Baba: Men and fatherhood in South Africa.* Cape Town: HSRC Press

Kalil A, Ziol-Guest KM & Coley RL (2005) Perception of father involvement patterns in teenage mother families: Predictors and links to mothers' psychological adjustment. *Family Relations* 54: 197–211

Kiselica MS (1995) *Multicultural counseling with teenage fathers: A practical guide.* Thousand Oaks, CA: Sage Publications

Kiselica MS & Sturmer P (1993) Is society giving teenage fathers a mixed message? *Youth & Society* 24(4): 487–501

Krishnakumar A & Black MM (2003) Family processes within three-generation households and adolescent mothers' satisfaction with father involvement. *Journal of Family Psychology* 17: 488–498

Lane TS & Clay CM (2000) Meeting the service needs of young fathers. *Child & Adolescent Social Work Journal* 17(1): 35–54

Lerman RI (1986) Who are the young absent fathers? *Youth & Society* 18(1): 3–27

Lesejane D (2006) Fatherhood from an African cultural perspective. In L Richter & R Morrell (eds) *Baba: Men and fatherhood in South Africa.* Cape Town: HSRC Press

Lesser J, Tello J, Koniak-Griffin D, Kappos B & Rhys M (2001) Young Latino fathers' perceptions of paternal role and risk for HIV/AIDS. *Hispanic Journal of Behavioral Sciences* 23(3): 327–343

Luttrell W (2003) *Pregnant bodies, fertile minds: Gender, race, and the schooling of pregnant teens.* New York: Routledge

Lynch K (1999) Equality studies, the academy and the role of research in emancipatory social change. *Economic and Social Review* 30(1): 41–69

Makiwane M & Udjo E (2006) *Is the child support grant associated with an increase in teenage fertility in South Africa? Evidence from national surveys and administrative data.* Pretoria: Human Sciences Research Council

Males M & Chew KSY (1996) The ages of fathers in California adolescent births, 1993. *American Journal of Public Health* 86(4): 565–568

Marsiglio W (1986) Teenage fatherhood: High school completion and educational attainment. In AB Elster & ME Lamb (eds) *Adolescent fatherhood.* Hillsdale, NJ: Lawrence Erlbaum Associates

Marsiglio W (1994) Young non-resident biological fathers. *Marriage & Family Review* 20(3/4): 325–348

Maxwell JA (1996) *Qualitative research design: An interactive approach.* Thousand Oaks, CA: Sage Publications

McAdoo JL (1990) Understanding African-American teen fathers. In PE Leone (ed.) *Understanding troubled and troubling youth.* Thousand Oaks, CA: Sage Publications

McAdoo JL (1993) The roles of African American fathers: An ecological perspective. *Families in Society* 74: 28–35

Milkie MA, Simon RW & Powell B (1997) Through the eyes of children: Youths' perceptions and evaluations of maternal and paternal roles. *Social Psychology Quarterly* 60(33): 218–237

Miller DB (1997) Adolescent fathers: What we know and what we need to know. *Child & Adolescent Social Work Journal* 14(1): 55–69

Miller-Johnson S, Winn DMC, Cole JD, Malone PS & Lochman J (2004) Risk factors for adolescent pregnancy reports among African American males. *Journal of Research on Adolescence* 14(4): 471–495

Mirza HS (1993) The social construction of black womanhood in British educational research. In M Arnot & K Weiler (eds) *Feminism and social justice in education: International perspectives.* Washington, DC: Falmer Press

Mkhize N (2006) African traditions and the social, economic and moral dimensions of fatherhood. In L Richter & R Morrell (eds) *Baba: Men and fatherhood in South Africa.* Cape Town: HSRC Press

Mollborn S (2006) *Understanding teenage pregnancy norms and their influence on teenage mothers' and fathers' life outcomes.* Dissertation, Stanford University. Available at http://gateway.proquest.com/openurl%3furl_ver=Z39.88-2004%26res_dat=xri:pqdiss%26rft_val_fmt=info:ofi/fmt:kev:mtx:dissertation%26rft_dat=xri:pqdiss:3219230. Accessed on 15 January 2009

Morrell R (2006) Fathers, fatherhood and masculinity in South Africa. In L Richter & R Morrell (eds) *Baba: Men and fatherhood in South Africa*. Cape Town: HSRC Press

Moultrie T & Dorrington R (2004) *Estimation of fertility from the 2001 South Africa Census data*. Cape Town: Centre for Actuarial Research, Statistics South Africa

Moultrie T & McGrath N (2007) Teenage fertility rates falling in South Africa. *South African Medical Journal* 97(6): 442–443

Moustakas C (1994) *Phenomenological research methods*. Thousand Oaks, CA: Sage Publications

Nagy S & Dunn MS (1999) Alcohol behaviors and deviant behaviors among adolescents in a rural state. *Journal of Alcohol & Drug Education* 44(3): 1–9

O'Connor ML (1998) Men who father children out of wedlock face reduced odds of marrying and increased socioeconomic hardship. *Family Planning Perspectives* 30(5): 248–249

Pears KC, Pierce SL, Kim HK, Capaldi DM & Owen LD (2005) The timing of entry into fatherhood in young, at-risk men. *Journal of Marriage and the Family* 67(2): 429–447

Pirog-Good MA (1996) The education and labor market outcomes of adolescent fathers. *Youth & Society* 28(2): 236–262

Posel D & Devey R (2006) The demographics of fatherhood in South Africa: An analysis of survey data, 1993–2002. In L Richter & R Morrell (eds) *Baba: Men and fatherhood in South Africa*. Cape Town: HSRC Press

Prata N, Vahidnia F & Fraser A (2005) Gender and relationship differences in condom use among 15–24-year-olds in Angola. *International Family Planning Perspectives* 31(4): 192–199

Pruett KD (1993) The paternal presence. *Families in Society* 74(1): 46–50

Purvez MSA (2003) *Making use of mediating resources: Social network of the extreme poor in Bangladesh*. Dhaka: Impact Monitoring and Evaluation Cell PROSHIKA

Quinton D, Pollock S & Anderson P (2002) *The transition to fatherhood in young men: Influences on commitment. Summary of key findings*. Bristol, UK: School for Policy Studies, Bristol University

Ramphele M (2002) *Steering by the stars: Being young in South Africa*. Cape Town: Tafelberg

Ramphele M & Richter L (2006) Migrancy, family dissolution and fatherhood. In L Richter & R Morrell (eds) *Baba: Men and fatherhood in South Africa*. Cape Town: HSRC Press

Reeves J (2007) 'Tell me your story': Applied ethics in narrative research with young fathers. *Children's Geographies* 5(3): 253–265

Resnick MD, Chambliss SA & Blum RW (1993) Health and risk behaviors of urban adolescent males involved in pregnancy. *Families in Society* 74(6): 366–374

Rhein LM, Ginsburg KR, Schwarz DF, Pinto-Martin JA, Zhao H, Morgan AP & Slap GB (1997) Teen father participation in child rearing: Family perspectives. *Journal of Adolescent Health* 21(4): 244–252

Rhoden JL & Robinson BE (1997) Teen dads: A generative fathering perspective versus the deficit myth. In AJ Hawkins & DC Dollahite (eds) *Generative fathering: Beyond deficit perspectives*. Thousand Oaks, CA: Sage Publications

Richter L & Morrell R (eds) (2006) *Baba: Men and fatherhood in South Africa*. Cape Town: HSRC Press

Richter L, Dawes A & Higson-Smith C (2004) *Sexual abuse of young children in southern Africa*. Cape Town: HSRC Press

Rivara FP, Sweeney PJ & Henderson BF (1985) A study of low socioeconomic status, black teenage fathers and their nonfather peers. *Pediatrics* 75(4): 648–656

Robinson BE (1988) Teenage pregnancy from the father's perspective. *American Journal of Orthopsychiatry* 58(1): 46–51

Santelli JS, Robin L, Brener ND & Lowry R (2001) Timing of alcohol and other drug use and sexual risk behaviors among unmarried adolescents and young adults. *Family Planning Perspectives* 33(5): 200–205

Shisana O, Rehle T, Simbayi LC, Parker W, Zuma K, Bhana A, Connoly C, Jooste S & Piillay V (2005) *South African national HIV prevalence, HIV incidence, behaviour and communication survey, 2005*. Cape Town: HSRC Press

Sibanda A (2004) Who drops out of school in South Africa? The influence of individual and household characteristics. *African Population Studies* 19(1): 99–116

Simbayi LC, Chauveau J & Shisana O (2004) Behavioural responses of South African youth to the HIV/AIDS epidemic: A nationwide survey. *AIDS Care* 16(5): 605–618

Smith PB, Buzi RS, Weinman ML & Mumford DM (2001) The use of focus groups to identify needs and expectations of young fathers in a male involvement program. *Journal of Sex Education & Therapy* 26(2): 100–105

Stueve A & O'Donnell LN (2005) Early alcohol initiation and subsequent sexual and alcohol risk behaviors among urban youths. *American Journal of Public Health* 95(5): 887–893

Sturgess W, Dunn J & Davies L (2001) Young children's perceptions of their relationships with family members: Links with family setting, friendships, and adjustment. *International Journal of Behavioral Development* 25(6): 521–529

Swartz S (2007) The moral ecology of South Africa's township youth. PhD thesis, University of Cambridge, UK

Swartz S (2009) *The moral ecology of South Africa's township youth.* New York: Palgrave Macmillan

Terreblanche SJ (2002) *A history of inequality in South Africa, 1652–2002.* Pietermaritzburg: University of KwaZulu-Natal Press

Thornberry TP, Smith CA & Howard GJ (1997) Risk factors for teenage fatherhood. *Journal of Marriage & Family* 59(3): 505–522

Veneziano RA & Rohner RP (1998) Perceived paternal acceptance, paternal involvement, and youths' psychological adjustment in a rural, biracial southern community. *Journal of Marriage & Family* 60(2): 335–343

Wei EH, Loeber R & Stouthamer-Loeber M (2002) How many of the offspring born to teenage fathers are produced by repeat serious delinquents? *Criminal Behaviour & Mental Health* 12(1): 83–98

Weinman ML, Buzi RS & Smith PB (2005) Addressing risk behaviours, service needs and mental health issues in programs for young fathers. *Families in Society* 86(2): 261–266

Weinman ML, Smith PB & Buzi RS (2002) Young fathers: An analysis of risk behaviors and service needs. *Child & Adolescent Social Work Journal* 19(6): 437–453

Wilson F (2006) On being a father and poor in South Africa today. In L Richter & R Morrell (eds) *Baba: Men and fatherhood in South Africa.* Cape Town: HSRC Press

Winstanley MR, Meyers SA & Florsheim P (2002) Psychosocial correlates of intimacy achievement among adolescent fathers-to-be. *Journal of Youth & Adolescence* 31(2): 91–100

Yasui M & Dishion TJ (2007) The ethnic context of child and adolescent problem behavior: Implications for child and family interventions. *Clinical Child and Family Psychology Review* 10(2): 137–179

About the authors

Dr Sharlene Swartz is a sociologist and researcher at the Child, Youth Family and Social Development research programme of the Human Sciences Research Council, and a visiting research fellow at the University of Cambridge.

Professor Arvin Bhana is a psychologist and the deputy Executive Director at the Child, Youth Family and Social Development research programme of the Human Sciences Research Council, and an adjunct associate professor in the School of Psychology at the University of KwaZulu-Natal.

About the CYFSD research programme at the HSRC

The Child, Youth, Family and Social Development (CYFSD) research programme of the HSRC aims to promote human and social development through the production of high quality applied research that addresses challenges arising from social inequality, poverty, violence, HIV/AIDS and other causes of ill-health and suffering, and loss of human potential. We research aspects of the life course, from infancy to old age, with an emphasis on understanding how contexts, policies and politics shape and distribute life chances. Throughout the life cycle, people learn, interact and develop within families, social and cultural groups, schools, workplaces, communities, and the economic, political and social orders. Our research focuses on individuals, groups and institutions relating to children, youth, families, and vulnerable populations, including older individuals and people with disabilities.